# THE INERT GASES
## MODEL SYSTEMS FOR SCIENCE

# THE WYKEHAM SCIENCE SERIES

*General Editors:*

PROFESSOR SIR NEVILL MOTT, F.R.S.
Cavendish Professor of Physics
University of Cambridge

G. R. NOAKES
Formerly Senior Physics Master
Uppingham School

The aim of the Wykeham Science Series is to broaden the outlook of the advanced high school student and introduce the undergraduate to the present state of science as a university study. Each volume seeks to reinforce the link between school and university levels. The principal author is a university professor distinguished in the field assisted by an experienced sixth-form instructor.

# THE INERT GASES
# MODEL SYSTEMS FOR SCIENCE

B. L. Smith – University of Sussex

WYKEHAM PUBLICATIONS (LONDON) LTD
LONDON and WINCHESTER
SPRINGER-VERLAG NEW YORK INC.
1971

546.75
S 643

*Sole Distributor for the United States, Canada and Mexico*
SPRINGER-VERLAG NEW YORK INC./NEW YORK

*Cover illustration—Research laboratory at the University of Sussex. In the foreground Mr. T. Bricheno measures the vapour pressure of a solidified inert gas mixture. Behind him, Mr. D. H. Garside operates a mass spectrometer to determine the rate at which helium gas diffuses through silver.*

*ISBN 0-387-91078-6*

*Library of Congress Catalog Card Number 71-153870*

*First published 1971 by Wykeham Publications (London) Ltd.*

*Printed in Great Britain by Taylor & Francis Ltd.*
*10–14 Macklin Street, London, WC2B 5NF*

# PREFACE

HELIUM, neon, argon, krypton, xenon and radon sound like Biblical characters from the Old Testament. In fact, they are members of the inert gas group of chemical elements (group O of the periodic table), small amounts of which exist in every breath of air we take. Their great value in physics is that their properties may be represented by simple theoretical models. As gases, or condensed into liquids or solids, they provide ideal systems with which to develop the molecular theory of the structure and properties of matter. The main part of this book describes how the inert gases have become ' model systems for science '.

Research on the inert gases is very active at present and most of the studies described here have been carried out within the past decade. Many important applications have been found in different branches of science and technology. Later sections of the book include an account of the uses of the inert gases in biology, engineering, geology and medicine, and describe their recently discovered chemical properties.

It is hoped that this book will serve as an introduction to model-building in the sciences, and be useful for both undergraduate and sixth-form courses concerned with the structure and properties of matter.

I am grateful to several colleagues and friends for their help during the preparation of this manuscript, and to the authors noted for permission to reproduce illustrations from their work. It gives me considerable pleasure to acknowledge the continuous encouragement and support of my schoolmaster colleague, Mr J. Webb, in particular the many valuable contributions that he has made towards making the text more understandable.

*Lewes*                                                            B. L. SMITH
*March*, 1971

*To William Chatfield*

# SYMBOLS AND UNITS

THOSE symbols that are in frequent use throughout this book are listed below. Where the same symbol is used to represent more than one quantity the appropriate chapter numbers are given in brackets. Other symbols have limited use only: these are defined in the text where appropriate. Except where indicated, the subscripts $v$, $l$, $s$, $c$ and $0$ refer to values for the vapour, liquid and solid phases, and at the critical point and $T = 0$ K, respectively.

## SYMBOLS

$a$    constant in van der Waals equation (3), lattice spacing (5), correlation length (7)

$A$    surface area

$^{40}Ar$    and similar symbols. The superscript indicates mass number of the atom of the element

$b$    constant in van der Waals equation

$C_p$, $C_v$, $C_m$    specific heat capacity at constant pressure, volume, magnetization

$D$    diffusion coefficient (5), electric displacement (8)

$E$    energy; electric field (2, 8)

$F$    Helmholtz free energy

$g_v$; $g(r)$    Gibbs free energy per vacancy; molecular distribution function $(g(r) = \rho(r) - 1)$

$G$    Gibbs free energy

$h$    Planck's constant

$H$    enthalpy (3), Hamiltonian (6)

$k$, $k_T$, $k_s$    Boltzmann's constant, isothermal compressibility, adiabatic compressibility

$l$    orbital quantum number (1), phonon mean free path (5), crystal grain size (5)

$m$    mass of molecule, magnetic quantum number (2), electric dipole moment (2, 8)

$n$; $n_2$ (1, 2), $n_3$ (1, 2, 3)    principal quantum number (1, 2, 5), number of vacancies per $N$ atoms in a crystal (5), population of energy level (10), refractive index; two and three molecule distribution functions

| | |
|---|---|
| $N$; $N_A$ | number of molecules in system; Avogadro's constant |
| $p$ | pressure, $n=2$ atomic state (2, 9, 10), momentum (3, 6) |
| $P$ | electric polarization (8) |
| $Q$ | activation energy per mole (5), momentum (5, 6) |
| $r$, $r_o$ | intermolecular distance, spacing between atoms at $T=0$ K |
| $R$ | gas constant |
| $s$ | $n=1$ atomic state |
| $S$ | entropy |
| $T$, $T_c$ | thermodynamic temperature, critical temperature |
| $U$ | energy |
| $v$ | velocity |
| $V$ | volume, Verdet constant (8) |
| $Z$ | atomic number (1), force (6), partition function (6) |
| $\alpha$ | expansivity, polarizability (2, 8), critical specific heat capacity index (7) |
| $\beta$ | critical density index |
| $\gamma$ | $C_p/C_v$ ratio (3); Grüneisen parameter (5), critical compressibility index (7) |
| $\delta$ | critical isotherm index |
| $\epsilon$ | interatomic potential constant; energy of an atomic oscillator (eigenvalue) (5); relative permittivity (dielectric constant) (8) |
| $\eta$ | viscosity |
| $\Theta_D$, $\Theta_E$ | Debye and Einstein characteristic temperatures |
| $\lambda$; $\Lambda^*$ | mean free path (3), thermal conductivity (5); wavelength of light (8), quantum parameter |
| $\nu$ | frequency |
| $\rho$, $\rho(r)$, $\rho_n$, $\rho_s$ | density, radial distribution function, density of normal and superfluid helium |
| $\sigma$ | molecular diameter, type of molecular orbital (9) |
| $\Omega$ | magneto-optical constant |
| $\phi$ | potential energy |
| $\chi$ | susceptibility |
| $\omega$ | solid angle (3), frequency (8) |

# UNITS

SI units are used throughout this book. These are explained, for example, in the Royal Society booklet *Symbols, Signs, and Abbreviations* (1969). A list of basic SI units, together with derived units, prefixes, conversion factors and numerical values for the common basic constants are given below.

### Basic SI units

| Quantity | Name | Symbol |
|---|---|---|
| length | metre | m |
| mass | kilogramme | kg |
| time | second | s |
| electric current | ampere | A |
| thermodynamic temperature | kelvin | K |
| amount of substance | mole | mol |

### Derived SI units

| Quantity | Name | Symbol |
|---|---|---|
| force | newton | $N = kg\ m\ s^{-2}$ |
| energy | joule | $J = kg\ m^2\ s^{-2}$ |
| power | watt | $W = kg\ m^2\ s^{-3}$ |
| electric charge | coulomb | $C = A\ s$ |
| electric potential difference | volt | $V = J\ A^{-1}\ s^{-1}$ |
| magnetic flux | weber | $Wb = V\ s$ |
| magnetic induction | tesla | $T = V\ s\ m^{-2}$ |
| frequency | hertz | $Hz = s^{-1}$ |
| velocity | metre per second | $m\ s^{-1}$ |
| acceleration | metre per second$^2$ | $m\ s^{-2}$ |
| electric intensity | volt per metre | $V\ m^{-1}$ |

### Prefixes for SI units

| Multiple | Prefix | Symbol | Multiple | Prefix | Symbol |
|---|---|---|---|---|---|
| $10^{-12}$ | pico | p | $10^3$ | kilo | k |
| $10^{-9}$ | nano | n | $10^6$ | mega | M |
| $10^{-6}$ | micro | $\mu$ | $10^9$ | giga | G |
| $10^{-3}$ | milli | m | $10^{12}$ | tera | T |

### Physical constants

| | | |
|---|---|---|
| $c$ | velocity of light | $3 \cdot 00 \times 10^8\ m\ s^{-1}$ |
| $h$ | Planck's constant | $6 \cdot 62 \times 10^{-34}\ J\ s$ |
| $k$ | Boltzmann's constant | $1 \cdot 38 \times 10^{-23}\ J\ K^{-1}$ |
| $N_A$ | Avogadro constant | $6 \cdot 02 \times 10^{23}\ mol^{-1}$ |
| $R$ | gas constant | $8 \cdot 30 \times 10^3\ J\ K^{-1}\ kg^{-1}$ |

### Conversion Factors

| | |
|---|---|
| angström | $1\ \text{Å} \equiv 10^{-10}\ m$ |
| atmosphere | $1\ atm \equiv 101 \cdot 3\ kN\ m^{-2}$ |
| barn | $1\ barn \equiv 10^{-28}\ m^2$ |
| electron-volt | $1\ eV \equiv 1 \cdot 60 \times 10^{-19}\ J$ |

# CONTENTS

## 1.1. *Introduction*

MORE than seventy years ago the discovery of the inert gases, otherwise known as ' noble ' or ' rare ' gases, caused a considerable stir in scientific circles. Their existence upset the ideas then current concerning the composition of the atmosphere, and the periodic classification of the elements. Once these difficulties had been settled, however, scientists soon lost interest in these gases. There were more exciting substances for the physicist and chemist to study. It is only within the past two decades that the inert gases have been rediscovered as valuable materials for research. It is interesting to note that it is generally just those properties that made them appear so dull and uninteresting to the pioneer scientist that today commend their study to the modern physicist.

Argon was the first of the inert gases to be discovered. Shortly before the turn of the century, Lord Rayleigh (fig. 1.1), an English physicist, set out to redetermine the densities of the principal gases then known. The measurements were considered to be routine, and Rayleigh did not anticipate that the investigation would lead to any startling results. Still less did he suspect that the work would lead to the discovery of a new element, for which he and his colleague, Sir William Ramsay, would be awarded Nobel Prizes.

The results of Rayleigh's experiments were consistent, except for nitrogen. Atmospheric nitrogen was found to be slightly more dense than nitrogen produced chemically. At this stage Rayleigh was joined in his researches by Ramsay, and the two men investigated the discrepancy. They found that the difference was due to the presence in atmospheric nitrogen of about 1% of an unknown element, which they named argon (Greek—non-active) because of its apparent inertness. In 1895, Rayleigh and Ramsay announced their discovery to a meeting of the Royal Society in London.

Their news was greeted with a certain amount of scepticism. At that time it was commonly supposed that air consisted of nitrogen, oxygen, carbon dioxide, and water vapour. Scientists had forgotten the work carried out by the chemist, Henry Cavendish, more than a century earlier. Cavendish had experimented to see whether ' phlogisticated air ' (nitrogen) was homogeneous or a mixture of different gases. He had found a small bubble of gas—presumably mainly argon—for which he could not account. but had concluded his investigation with the

1

Fig. 1.1.  Lord Rayleigh (left) and Lord Kelvin in the laboratory ($\sim$1900).

comment, '. . . if there be any part of the phlogisticated air of our atmosphere which differs from the rest, we may safely conclude that it is not more than 1/120 part of the whole.'

Another upsetting factor which made scientsts unprepared to accept the existence of argon was that it did not fit into the periodic table. The properties of argon were such that it did not correspond to any of the elements which scientists predicted would be brought to light because of the gaps left in the table.

The controversy was ended with the subsequent discovery of helium, neon, and the other inert gases. It was then realized that these gases formed an entirely new group in the periodic table (group O)—elements which were characterized by complete chemical inactivity.

Apart from radon, which is radioactive, and helium, which exhibits unusual properties at low temperatures, the inert gases had little obvious appeal as materials for research. In recent years, however, there has been a revival of interest in these substances because of the realization that they closely correspond to simple theoretical models, and are therefore useful in the development of molecular theory.

One of the most ambitious programmes in which physicists and chemists are now engaged is the development of the molecular theory of the physical properties of matter. Their aim is to describe the macroscopic or 'real-life' properties of gases, liquids, and solids, in terms of molecular behaviour. In general, this is an impossible task because of the complicated mathematics involved; but for certan substances, of which the inert gases are outstanding examples, enough simplifying assumptions may be made for the development of such a theory to be possible.

For example, when calculating a macroscopic property, one should, in principle, consider the contributions made to the property by each of the molecules. It is, in other words, a 'many-body' problem involving all $N$ of the molecules, where for a sample of say 1 kg, $N$ is about $10^{25}$. This, of course, takes a long time to compute! Fortunately, the problem can be simplified somewhat for the inert gases.

The forces which act between inert gas molecules, and which bind them together in the liquid and solid states, are short-range and effective only over a distance of a few molecular diameters. They are also expressible in simple algebraic terms. The net force acting on any one molecule can therefore be accurately estimated by considering inter-actions with its nearer neighbours only. Molecules further away than a few molecular diameters will make no contribution. The net force operating on the representative molecule can be expressed as a 'two-body' force, acting between the molecule on one hand and its neighbours on the other.

The bulk property is then obtained by adding up these effects for all the molecules which are present, assuming that the net forces acting on them are the same as for the representative molecule.

This type of calculation is relatively easy for the inert gases because the effect of 'free' electrons does not have to be taken into considera-tion. The atoms are characterized by full and stable electron shells, and this is what gives them their inert properties. They are in fact like the miniature 'ping-pong balls' often used in scientific theories—easy to handle mathematically because they are spherically symmetrical in their interactions.

The inert gases, with the exception of helium, are readily liquefied

3

| | Boiling point (K) (at 101 kN m$^{-2}$ pressure) | Triple point (K) |
|---|---|---|
| Helium | 4·2 | — |
| Neon | 26·3 | 24·5 |
| Argon | 87·3 | 83·8 |
| Krypton | 120·3 | 116·1 |
| Xenon | 165·2 | 161·4 |
| Radon | ∼211·0 | ∼202·0 |

Table 1.1.  Boiling points and triple points of the inert gases.

and solidified by normal low temperature methods (Table 1.1). They may therefore be investigated as gases, liquids, or solids. Argon is the obvious inert gas to study because it is available in a high degree of purity and from the standpoint of liquid and solid state experiments, condenses in a convenient temperature range. Neon has a high zero-point energy to total energy ratio (see § 2.4) so that quantum effects are relatively more important than in the heavier inert gases, and krypton and xenon are considerably more expensive because of their relative rarity. Radon is radioactive and helium displays quantum rather than classical behaviour. Another advantage in research applications is that argon when extracted from the atmosphere consists nearly entirely (99·6%) of a single isotope $^{40}$Ar, whereas both natural krypton and xenon are mixtures of appreciable quantities of several different isotopes.

In the condensed state the inert gases form colourless liquids and, under suitable conditions, freeze into compact transparent solids. This book is concerned mainly with the ' classical ' properties of gases, liquids and solids and the treatments given for liquids and solids are therefore not as a rule applicable to helium except where mentioned. Neon, although showing some deviations from classical behaviour, may be included, at least to a first approximation, with the heavier inert gases.

## 1.2. *Occurrence and origin*

All the inert gases are found throughout most of the Universe. The relative abundance may be estimated on the basis of spectroscopic evidence and the analysis of rock and meteorite samples (see § 10.2). The estimated concentrations in the Universe, the earth's crust and the earth's atmosphere are shown in Table 1.2. In the case of the first two, the abundances are quoted relative to silicon. Silicon provides a useful standard because it forms stable, non-volatile compounds and was probably not lost during the evolution of the earth.

Hydrogen and helium are the most common elements in the Universe. The sun, stars, and some of the major planets such as Jupiter and Saturn consist mostly of these gases. It has been estimated that at present

|     | Atomic abundance in earth's crust | Atomic abundance in Universe | Volume concentration in dry air |
| --- | --- | --- | --- |
| He | $2 \cdot 2 \times 10^{-7}$ | $3 \cdot 1 \times 10^{3}$ | $5 \cdot 2 \times 10^{-6}$ |
| Ne | $2 \cdot 7 \times 10^{-8}$ | $8 \cdot 7$ | $1 \cdot 8 \times 10^{-5}$ |
| Ar | $9 \cdot 4 \times 10^{-6}$ | $1 \cdot 5 \times 10^{-1}$ | $0 \cdot 93$ |
| Kr | $2 \cdot 5 \times 10^{-10}$ | $5 \cdot 1 \times 10^{-5}$ | $1 \cdot 1 \times 10^{-6}$ |
| Xe | $2 \cdot 4 \times 10^{-11}$ | $4 \cdot 0 \times 10^{-6}$ | $8 \cdot 6 \times 10^{-8}$ |
| Rn | $2 \quad \times 10^{-19}$ | — | $6 \times 10^{-20}$ |

Table 1.2. Relative abundances of inert gases in the Earth's crust, the Universe and air. The first two columns refer to numbers of atoms relative to 1 atom of silicon, the third is the volume fraction content of dry air.

about 76% of the mass of the Universe is hydrogen and 23% is helium. All the other elements combined account for less than 1% of the total mass.

Only about 0·02% of the inert gases associated with the earth are in the atmosphere. The rest are occluded in rocks or dissolved in water. However, with the possible exception of helium, the concentration in minerals is too low for commercial recovery. The inert gases contained in the earth's crust are gradually liberated by weathering processes and by diffusion. Natural gas deposits, volcanic gases and hot springs contain a relatively high abundance of these gases. The natural gas deposits provide the most important source of helium, concentrations of as high as 8 mole per cent being found in some wells.

The composition of the earth's atmosphere has probably remained essentially constant during the past $10^9$ years, although there is some evidence that the concentration of the $^{40}$Ar isotope is slowly increasing due to decay of $^{40}$K (see § 10.2). The gravitational field of the earth is sufficiently strong to hold all gas molecules heavier than helium. A steady state has been reached in which the $^3$He and $^4$He emerging into the atmosphere from natural sources is balanced by their escape into interstellar space.

The origin of the inert gases is closely linked with the origin of the Universe and as such is still controversial. However, some basic features are reasonably well established. At the starting point of the Universe a mass of either neutrons or hydrogen gas was present. In the case of neutrons, these would rapidly decay to protons and electrons and thus be equivalent to hydrogen atoms.

The hydrogen condensed to form stars, under conditions of high pressure and temperature, in which elements heavier than hydrogen were synthesized. This process is still occurring in stars. The types of reaction that can take place between nuclear particles under these

5

conditions are as follows:

$$\text{proton} + \text{proton} \rightarrow \text{deuteron} + \text{positron} + \text{neutrino}$$

$$\text{deuteron} + \text{proton} \rightarrow {}^3\text{He}$$

$${}^3\text{He} + {}^3\text{He} \rightarrow {}^4\text{He} + 2 \text{ protons}$$

$${}^4\text{He} + {}^4\text{He} + {}^4\text{He} \rightarrow {}^{12}\text{C}$$

$${}^{12}\text{C} + {}^4\text{He} \rightarrow {}^{16}\text{O}$$

$${}^{16}\text{O} + {}^4\text{He} \rightarrow {}^{20}\text{Ne}$$

${}^3\text{He}$ is the lighter helium isotope of mass number 3, a deuteron is the nucleus of a deuterium (heavy hydrogen) atom and consists of one proton plus one neutron, a positron is a particle of the same mass as an electron but with a positive charge, and a neutrino is a particle of negligible mass or charge but with a nuclear spin of $\frac{1}{2}$.

The first three interactions can take place in compressed hydrogen at about $5 \times 10^6$ K. The synthesis of ${}^{12}\text{C}$ from three ${}^4\text{He}$ atoms requires a temperature of $10^8$ K. As the star contracts it is believed that still higher temperatures ($\sim 5 \times 10^9$ K) occur and that other nuclear reactions take place which result in the formation of elements of mass number up to about 56 (Fe). Finally, the star explodes, and the material is thrown into interstellar space, where 'second-generation' stars are formed.

The second-generation stars consist mainly of hydrogen, but also contain portions of some of the heavier elements, of mass numbers up to 56, that were produced in the original stars. At this stage the carbon–nitrogen cycle operates, in which, starting from ${}^{12}\text{C}$, ${}^{14}\text{N}$ and ${}^{15}\text{N}$ are formed by proton capture. Some of the ${}^{15}\text{N}$ reacts with protons to return to ${}^{12}\text{C}$. Also taking place are reactions which result in the release of neutrons. Some of the neutrons are captured by nuclei to form heavier isotopes, for example,

$${}^{20}\text{Ne} + \text{neutron} \rightarrow {}^{21}\text{Ne}; \text{ and } {}^{21}\text{Ne} + \text{neutron} \rightarrow {}^{22}\text{Ne}$$

As the nuclei of these isotopes become increasingly heavy by successive neutron capture, they eventually become unstable and disintegrate, ejecting one or more charged particles in the process, thus forming new elements.

The main sources of the inert gases in the atmosphere are summarized in Table 1.3. Except for a little helium formed directly in the atmosphere, or entering it from interstellar space, most of the isotopes emanate from the earth's crust. Small quantities of ${}^4\text{He}$, ${}^{40}\text{Ar}$ and radon are continuously being produced by radio-active decay (see fig. 10.2, § 10.2) and on a much smaller scale, krypton and xenon result from the fission of uranium and thorium. The production and decay of radon, like the supply and escape of helium, are roughly

6

| | Origin |
|---|---|
| $^3$He | Decay of tritium ($^3$H) in the atmosphere. |
| $^4$He | Alpha particles entering the atmosphere in cosmic radiation, or by decay of radioactive elements. |
| Ne, Ar, Kr, Xe | Mostly primordial in origin and released from rocks etc. by weathering and other action.   Very small amounts produced by nuclear reactions. |
| $^{40}$Ar | Radioactive decay of $^{40}$K. |
| Rn | Radioactive decay of radium. |

Table 1.3.   Main sources of inert gases in the Earth's atmosphere.

| | Mass number of isotope | Relative abundance, per cent |
|---|---|---|
| He | 3<br>4 | $1 \cdot 3 \times 10^{-4}$<br>$\sim 100$ |
| Ne | 20<br>21<br>22 | $90 \cdot 9$<br>$0 \cdot 3$<br>$8 \cdot 8$ |
| Ar | 36<br>38<br>40 | $0 \cdot 34$<br>$6 \times 10^{-2}$<br>$99 \cdot 6$ |
| Kr | 78<br>80<br>82<br>83<br>84<br>86 | $0 \cdot 4$<br>$2 \cdot 3$<br>$11 \cdot 6$<br>$11 \cdot 6$<br>$56 \cdot 9$<br>$17 \cdot 3$ |
| Xe | 124<br>126<br>128<br>129<br>130<br>131<br>132<br>134<br>136 | $0 \cdot 1$<br>$0 \cdot 1$<br>$1 \cdot 9$<br>$26 \cdot 4$<br>$4 \cdot 1$<br>$21 \cdot 2$<br>$26 \cdot 9$<br>$10 \cdot 4$<br>$8 \cdot 9$ |

Table 1.4.   Relative abundance of stable inert gas isotopes in the atmosphere.

balanced so that the concentration of these gases in the atmosphere remains essentially constant.

It is believed that all $^3$He originates from the decay of tritium ($^3$H), created in nuclear reactions triggered off by cosmic rays. Most of the neon on earth and the $^{36}$Ar and $^{38}$Ar isotopes are probably of primordial origin. The relative abundances of the stable inert gas isotopes are given in Table 1.4.

## 1.3. *Extraction of the inert gases*

Most of the stable isotopes of argon, neon, krypton and xenon are produced *via* the liquefaction of air. Helium is extracted from natural gas sources, located mainly in the U.S.A. The concentration of helium in the air is relatively low, so that at present it is not commercially practicable to separate helium from the air in bulk, except in the course of producing krypton and xenon. The composition of the atmosphere is given in Table 1.5. In addition to the permanent gases listed there are quantities of water vapour, ozone and other compounds, depending on the position at which the sample is taken.

| Gas | Percentage composition (atomic) |
|---|---|
| N$_2$ | 78·08 |
| O$_2$ | 20·95 |
| Ar | 0·93 |
| CO$_2$ | 0·03 |
| Rare gases | 0·003 |

Table 1.5. The composition of dry (pure) air.

There are two main stages in the extraction of inert gases from the air—liquefaction and separation. Liquefaction is carried out by compressing air and then allowing it to expand through a nozzle. This cools the air (by the Joule–Thomson effect) until it begins to condense. A second method that is often combined with Joule–Thomson cooling in commercial refrigeration plants is to let part of the compressed air drive an expansion engine; the combined effects provide a more convenient and efficient method of cooling than either on its own.

Liquid air is separated into its components by fractional distillation in a tall rectifier. In practice it is found that a double rectifier system in which one column is placed above a second maintained at a slightly higher temperature and pressure provides the most efficient arrangement. Both rectifiers contain a large number of metal trays, each with a large number of perforations in it. Liquid and vapour flow freely through the holes. Enriched portions of gas or liquid may be extracted *via* valves at various parts of the columns. For example, argon vapour is withdrawn at a point in the upper column where it is at a concentration of about 12%. Uncondensed neon, helium and hydrogen collect in the condenser and may be withdrawn for subsequent purification.

The 12% enriched argon is passed through a second fractionating column where the concentration is increased to ~98%. A combination of combustion (to remove the oxygen), differential absorption, and other techniques, may then be used to produce argon of a purity of 99·996% or better. The neon–helium mixture is concentrated by fractional distillation and then separated by passing the mixture over cooled charcoal. This adsorbs nearly all the neon but very little of the helium.

Krypton and xenon are generally separated from the liquid oxygen portion of the fractionating column and then concentrated by a series of liquefaction and distillation steps, followed by adsorption and desorption on charcoal. The process is a lengthy one and if it was not for the commercial importance of oxygen, and argon, and hence the extraction of these gases in large quantities, krypton and xenon would be much rarer and more expensive than they are. It requires about sixty million litres of air to produce enough xenon for a single reasonably sized sample of solid.

## 1.4. *Electronic structure*

Atoms consist of a minute nucleus around which a number of electrons circulate. In the Bohr model of the atom (fig. 1.2(a)) these occupy well defined orbits and may be thought of as small negatively charged particles. The modern quantum mechanical approach has modified this picture. The electron particle is replaced by a cloud-like charge distribution in which the density of the cloud represents the probability of finding an electron. The maximum probability corresponds to the old Bohr orbit (fig. 1.2(b)).

The nucleus consists of uncharged neutrons and positively charged protons, and the number of electrons associated with an unionised atom is equal to the atomic number $Z$—the number of protons in the nucleus.

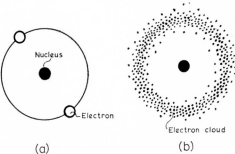

(a)                                      (b)

Fig. 1.2. (a) Representation of a helium atom on Bohr model. (b) Quantum mechanical representation of helium atom.

9

The chemical properties of an atom are determined by the electron configuration, particularly that of the outermost shells.

The electrons surrounding the nucleus of a neutral atom fall into certain well defined orbits and energy levels, and the stable arrangement is governed by certain quantum mechanical rules. In general an electron is assigned four quantum numbers to describe its state, and, according to the Pauli exclusion principle, not more than one electron in an atom may have a given set of quantum numbers. When determining the electron distribution in an atom of atomic number $Z$, therefore, the procedure is to fill up each shell with electrons of different quantum numbers, starting with the lowest energy level, to a total of $Z$ electrons.

The lowest energy level has a principal quantum number, $n$, of 1. In this configuration the electron distribution about the nucleus is spherically symmetrical and there is no angular momentum. It is designated the $1s$ state. It is possible, however, to consider two possible spin states of an electron, one in which the spin points in a given direction, say $\uparrow$, and the other in which the spin is opposite, i.e. $\downarrow$. These have different spin quantum numbers and hence it is possible to have two electrons in the $1s$ state, of opposite spin.

The second shell has a principal quantum number $n = 2$. The lowest level is again spherically symmetrical ($2s$ state) and can contain two electrons of opposite spin. But there is also a higher energy orbit, which is dumb-bell in shape. This may have angular momentum in three possible directions, each of which may contain two electrons. By this process one arrives at a set of rules for defining and assigning quantum numbers as given in Table 1.6.

|  |  | Possible values |
|---|---|---|
| Principal quantum number | $n$ | 1, 2, 3, ... |
| Orbital quantum number | $l$ | 0, 1, ..., $(n-1)$ |
| Magnetic quantum number | $m$ | $l$, $(l-1)$, ..., $-l$ |
| Spin quantum number | $s$ | $-\frac{1}{2}$ or $+\frac{1}{2}$ |

Table 1.6. Possible values of quantum numbers. According to the Pauli exclusion principle, no two electrons in an atom may have the same four quantum numbers.

The outermost electrons, particularly those with unpaired spins determine the chemical properties of an atom. The distribution of electrons in the inert gases (Table 1.7) are characterized by full and stable outer shells, and this is the primary reason for their inert properties. It is only very recently that it has been discovered that under very

10

| Principal quantum number, $n$ | 1 | 2 | 3 | 4 | 5 | 6 |
|---|---|---|---|---|---|---|
| Atomic number | Number of electrons in quantum level | | | | | |

| | Atomic number | 1 | 2 | 3 | 4 | 5 | 6 |
|---|---|---|---|---|---|---|---|
| He | 2 | 2 | — | — | — | — | — |
| Ne | 10 | 2 | 8 | — | — | — | — |
| Ar | 18 | 2 | 8 | 8 | — | — | — |
| Kr | 36 | 2 | 8 | 18 | 8 | — | — |
| Xe | 54 | 2 | 8 | 18 | 18 | 8 | — |
| Rn | 86 | 2 | 8 | 18 | 32 | 18 | 8 |

Table 1.7.   Arrangement of electrons in group O elements.

favourable conditions, some of the inert gases may be made to form stable chemical compounds, for example, xenon hexafluoride (see Chapter 9).   However, for the purposes of most of this book they may be regarded as stable chemically inert atoms, spherically symmetrical in their interactions.

The inert gases are monatomic and therefore their ' atomic ' properties are identical with their ' molecular ' properties.

## 1.5. *Properties of liquid helium*

Those sections of this book that are devoted to condensed state properties of the inert gases are primarily concerned with the heavier gases, because these form ' well-behaved ' liquids and solids, to which the laws of classical physics may reasonably be applied.   Helium, on the other hand, with its relatively high zero-point energy (see § 2.4) becomes a ' quantum fluid ' at low temperatures, and exhibits some quite unusual experimental properties.

Helium-4 gas condenses at about 4·2 K to form a colourless liquid. If this is cooled, at about 2 K the liquid undergoes a ' second order ' phase change (the lambda transition) to another type of helium, known as liquid helium II.   Further cooling does not produce solid helium, however, because of the high ' zero-point vibrational energy ' (see § 2.4), which is sufficient to prevent the light helium molecules from forming a crystal lattice.   The liquid phase is stable even at the lowest temperatures, and, close to 0 K, a pressure of at least 2·5 MN m$^{-2}$ is required to overcome the vibrational energy sufficiently for solid helium to be formed.   The phase diagram for $^4$He is shown in fig. 2.12.

Associated with the lambda transition are some striking thermal anomalies, involving discontinuities in the expansivity ($\alpha$), molar specific heat capacity($C_p$) and compressibility ($k_T$).   The reason why the

11

transition is called a second order phase change is that each of these properties is a second derivative of the Gibbs free energy (see Appendix), i.e.

$$\alpha = \frac{1}{V}\left(\frac{\partial^2 G}{\partial T \partial p}\right), \quad C_p = -T\left(\frac{\partial^2 G}{\partial T^2}\right) \quad \text{and} \quad k_T = \frac{1}{V}\left(\frac{\partial^2 G}{\partial p^2}\right)$$

The lambda transition is similar in several respects to the vapour–liquid critical point except that it is a line in the $p$–$T$ plane rather than a single point. The extent to which the lambda transition is analogous to other critical phenomena is considered in § 7.7.

Liquid helium II exhibits many unusual properties and some of these are discussed below. To explain the properties of helium II, a 'two-fluid' theory has been proposed. On the basis of this theory, liquid helium is supposed to consist of two fluids, one a 'normal' fluid and the other a 'superfluid'. These both occupy the same physical space but operate independently of each other.

The normal fluid is responsible for the properties of helium II which one would usually associate with a liquid, for example, viscosity and specific heat. The superfluid on the other hand, has no viscosity or even entropy. It therefore does not contribute to the observed viscosity or to the specific heat capacity. The proportions of normal fluid and superfluid in helium II vary with temperature (fig. 1.3). As the

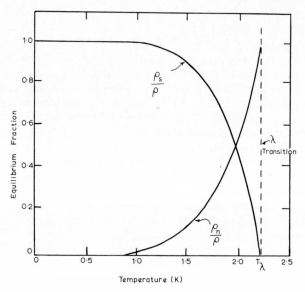

Fig. 1.3. Variation of the equilibrium proportions of normal and superfluid helium II with temperature. ($\rho$—total density of fluid. $\rho_s$—density of superfluid. $\rho_n$—density of normal fluid.)

temperature drops towards 0 K, the relative amount of the superfluid increases and that of the normal fluid decreases, until at absolute zero only superfluid is present. At a given temperature the density of helium II ($\rho$) is the sum of the density of the superfluid ($\rho_s$) and that of the normal fluid ($\rho_n$). Because the two fluids are non-interacting, it is possible to imagine that they can flow in the tube in opposite directions, each displaying its particular transport properties without regard to the presence of the other component. These properties are best illustrated by considering some of the curious effects observed during experiments with liquid helium.

Above the lambda transition, the viscosity of liquid helium, although low in value, varies with temperature from the critical temperature 5·3 K down to about 3 K in roughly the manner expected. Below this temperature, however, the viscosity decreases rapidly until at about 1 K it becomes effectively zero (fig. 1.4($a$)). In fact, the situation is more complicated, because below the lambda transition, different techniques yield different values for the viscosity. For example, the viscosity as

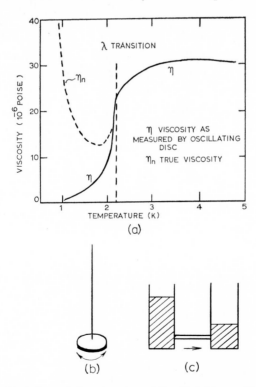

Fig. 1.4. ($a$) Variation of the viscosity of liquid helium with temperature. ($b$) Torsion disc method for determining the viscosity. ($c$) Capillary method for viscosity determinations.

determined by observing the damping of an oscillating disc (fig. 1.4(b)) varies with temperature as shown in fig. 1.4(a). However, values determined by noting the rate at which the liquid flows along a capillary tube under constant pressure conditions (fig. 1.4(c)), are quite different. In the latter experiment, tubes of diameter $> 10^{-4}$ m give results identical with those obtained in the oscillating disc experiment, whereas the flow in smaller diameter tubes appears to *increase*, rather than decrease, as the tube diameter is decreased. When the tube diameter is as small as $\sim 10^{-7}$ m a 'critical' velocity of about 0·13 m s$^{-1}$ is obtained. At this stage, the flow appears to be quite independent of the pressure difference between the ends of the tube.

Another striking effect is observed when a beaker is partially immersed in He II as shown in fig. 1.5(a). The empty beaker rapidly becomes covered with a thin film of the fluid. Helium then flows into the beaker until the level reaches that of the liquid outside. If the beaker is raised (fig. 1.5(b)), the flow reverses until the levels once more correspond. Even stranger, the rate of flow appears to be independent of both the path length and the difference in height between the two levels.

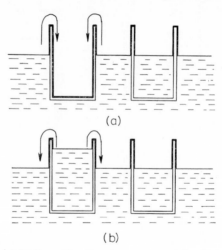

Fig. 1.5. (a) Helium film flow into an empty beaker. (b) Level recovery in helium II via film flow.

As in the case of the flow of helium II through small tubes, these effects are attributable to the superfluid. In the former case, the critical velocity is thought to mark the point at which the superfluid atoms have sufficient energy to interact significantly with the normal fluid. Flow via a helium film is attributed to the phenomenon of adsorption. Below the lambda transition, flow in the film by the mixture of normal and superfluid helium is thought to take place over a layer of solid helium two or three atoms thick. The probable existence

14

of such a solid layer is supported by calculations of the likely pressure within the film. This, surprisingly, turns out to be greater than the $2 \cdot 6$ MN m$^{-2}$ ($\sim 26$ atmospheres) required for the solid to form.

Above the lambda transition liquid helium has an average thermal conductivity of $\sim 10^{-3}$ J s$^{-1}$ m$^{-1}$ K$^{-1}$ which is considerably lower than typical values for other liquids. Below the lambda transition, however, the conductivity increases to a value some $2 \times 10^7$ higher than that of helium I. This is a factor of $10^3$ greater than that of copper at room temperature. The increase explains why helium appears to stop boiling when cooled below the lambda transition. Because of its huge thermal conductivity, the liquid distributes heat too quickly to allow bubble formation. All evaporation therefore takes place at the surface.

The actual mechanism of heat conduction in helium II is more complicated than that in ordinary fluids. For example, the heat flow is found to depend on the temperature gradient and geometry of the cell as well as on the temperature of the fluid. The highest conductivity is obtained in small capillaries under small temperature gradients. The two-fluid theory is able to provide an explanation for this. Heat conduction takes place by a circulation of the normal and superfluid components, in which the superfluid flows to warmer areas where it absorbs heat and becomes normal and the normal fluid flows in the opposite direction, at a rate governed by the viscosity. The circulation of the superfluid is extremely rapid because of its negligible viscosity. It is also able to absorb a considerable quantity of heat when it is transformed into normal helium II because it has no entropy.

These thermal properties are well demonstrated by the thermo-mechanical effect observed when two reservoirs are connected by a capillary as shown in fig. $1.6(a)$. When heat is passed into one of the

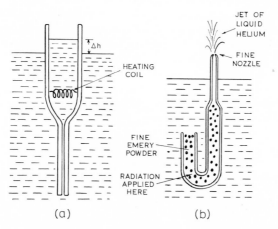

$$(a) \qquad\qquad (b)$$

Fig. 1.6. (a) Thermomechanical effect. (b) Fountain effect in liquid helium II.

reservoirs the level is seen to rise. This is due to superfluid flowing from the cooler of the reservoirs to the warmer. On reaching the warmer reservoir, the superfluid absorbs heat and turns normal, but because of the viscosity is unable to return.

The motion is shown even more effectively by the apparatus shown in fig. 1.6(b). The lower part of the glass tube is packed tightly with emery powder so that only superfluid is allowed to pass. When a light is focussed on to the tube, the emery powder absorbs radiation and becomes warmer than the rest of the apparatus. The resulting flow of superfluid is so rapid that liquid is expelled from the nozzle as a fountain.

There are many other interesting effects and experiments associated with superfluid helium. One experiment, for example, is designed to test the two-fluid theory of helium II and is based on the detection of ' second-sound ' within the fluid. In a normal substance, heat transferred by conduction is ' smeared out ' as it travels through the material. According to second-sound theory, however, a heat pulse can travel through superfluid helium without losing its thermal profile because the fluid has no entropy or heat capacity. The pulse advances by means of a sound wave type of propagation.

There are, of course, definite properties associated with waves. Before the second-sound theory of helium II was accepted, these characteristics had to be demonstrated for second-sound thermal waves. This has been achieved by producing a diffraction pattern using a number of thermal sources placed equal distances apart ( $\sim 5$ mm). Several orders of thermal intensity maxima were observed at angles to the thermal grating similar to those observed when X-rays are diffracted by a crystal. This wave-like behaviour presented striking evidence for the second-sound hypothesis.

A superfluid ' wind tunnel ' has recently been devised to test the principles of hydrodynamics. According to theory, bodies of arbitrary shape exposed to the flow of a perfect fluid will not experience ' lift ' or a net force, but only a torque. Utilizing the thermomechanical effect described above, helium II superfluid is made to flow past the suspended model of a wing assembly while the normal fluid remains stationary. The results of these tests confirm the theoretical predictions. Within certain limits of superfluid velocity no ' lift ' is observed on the wing assembly.

One experiment with superfluid helium is interesting because it provides a link with the past. A ' Rayleigh disc ' is used to measure the torque produced by second-sound waves in liquid helium II. This device works on the same principle as the disc which was invented by Lord Rayleigh before the turn of the century, and which was employed by him for refined acoustical measurements. It is appropriate that Rayleigh's name is still heard in the laboratory in connection with the inert gases, more than seventy years after his discovery of argon!

## 2.1. *Introduction*

A GREAT deal of the current effort in science is directed towards relating the real-life properties of gases, liquids and solids to behaviour at the atomic and molecular level. The object is to understand in terms of interatomic spacings and potentials, why substances in bulk, i.e. in large groups of atoms, behave as they do. Although it has made much progress recently, this subject is still at an elementary stage of development. Because the inert gases correspond well to relatively simple theoretical models, they provide ideal systems for study in such investigations.

How is a molecular theory developed? Basically, by a series of successive approximations, involving both the theoretician and the experimentalist. It starts with the assumption of a plausible microscopic model. Because it is impossible to see individual atoms, we have to assume what they look like.

A suitable model for a gas, for example, might be a large number of minute hard spheres in continuous motion, colliding frequently with the walls of the container and occasionally with each other. Using this model as a basis, a theoretician can compute the behaviour of the gas, its density, its thermal and transport properties, and its equation of state. These can then all be measured experimentally. If there is good agreement between the calculated and experimental results, then this model was a good choice. If, however, the results do not agree, then the obvious conclusion is that the model is not realistic. In this case, it has to be modified in some way and the calculations repeated.

In practice, the situation is usually not so clear-cut. At any one time there are both theoreticians and experimentalists studying a given property. As the theory evolves, many of the earlier experiments have to be repeated more accurately, so that the data are good enough to test a new hypothesis. Occasionally, there are rapid advances as revolutionary new ideas are formulated and tested. One complication that often arises is that a model which appears to give an excellent description of some properties, for instance density and specific heat capacity, fails hopelessly when it comes to others. For example, a 'hard-sphere' molecular model of a gas may provide quite an accurate description of the viscosity, but its optical properties invoke the electron energy levels within the atoms. Although the models that are discussed in this book are primarily of atomic scale and concern particles and distances $\sim 0.1$ nm in size, models are used to represent physical systems at many other levels, ranging from the nuclear ($\sim 10^{-15}$ m), to the astronomical ($\sim 10^{22}$ m).

## 2.2. *Gases, liquids and solids*

Using a collection of hard spheres to represent molecules, it is possible to make quite simple models that can reproduce most of the features of gases, liquids and solids. By examining these simple models in detail, one can then determine in what respects they fail, and hence modify them so that they become more valid.

What are the distinctive features of the gas phase, the liquid phase and the solid phase? Simple observation suggests that a solid can be defined as a system that can support a shear stress indefinitely. A liquid can act as if it had some mechanical rigidity for a short period but does flow, and therefore has to be placed in a container. A gas has to be kept in a container with a lid.

The density of a given substance in the liquid phase is about 0.8 of the density in the solid phase, but about $10^3$ times its density in the gas phase. The most rigid structure thus has the molecules closest together. The figures suggest that there are attractive forces between neighbouring molecules that vary inversely as some power of the distance, $r$, separating them, i.e., as $1/r^n$. In a gas where the typical average distance $r$ between molecules is about 3 nm, the attraction is negligible, but in both liquids and solids ($r \sim 0.3$ nm) the forces are sufficient to keep the molecules more or less ' glued ' together. The density is greatest when the molecules are packed closely together in the solid phase. Any further reduction of volume will be met with strong resistance from the ' hard-sphere ' molecules. This is in agreement with the experimental observation that gases are highly compressible but solids are not. A simple force curve can be drawn to describe how the interaction between two typical molecules varies with the separation $r$ (fig. 2.1).

How are the molecules distributed in gases, liquids and solids? This information can be obtained from the results of X-ray diffraction experiments. In a gas the molecules are found to be randomly distributed with typical average spacing of about 3 nm. The molecules in a solid, on the other hand, are on average only about 0.3 nm apart and are usually packed together in an orderly array on a crystalline lattice. A liquid has neither the molecular chaos of a gas, nor the long range order of a solid, but is a kind of intermediate case (fig. 2.2).

Consider a typical molecule $(X)$, within a substance, fig. 2.3($a$). The distribution of the other molecules relative to it may be described in terms of the radial distribution function $\rho(r)$. This is defined such that $\rho(r)\mathrm{d}r$ represents the probability of finding another molecule between $r$ and $r + \mathrm{d}r$ from the centre of $X$. In fig. 2.3($a$), which shows a two-dimensional square lattice, the *nearest neighbours* to $X$ lie at a distance

18

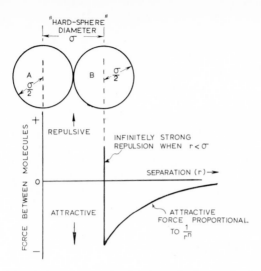

Fig. 2.1. Simple force curve showing how the interaction between two hard-sphere molecules varies with their separation.

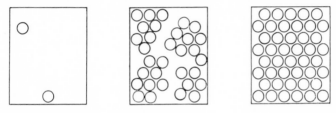

Fig. 2.2. Comparison of the molecular distributions in a gas, a liquid and a solid.

$r = a$. There are four nearest neighbours shown in fig. 2.3(*a*), four second nearest neighbours, eight third nearest neighbours and so on, fig. 2.3(*b*). Real substances are three-dimensional, of course, and a molecule in a three-dimensional (cubic) lattice has six nearest neighbours. Because the number of molecules lying in a shell between $r$ and $r + \mathrm{d}r$ increases rapidly as $r$ becomes larger it is more convenient to use the reduced distribution function $g(r)$, defined by $g(r) = \rho(r)/4\pi r^2$. Typical reduced distributions for a gas, a liquid and a solid are shown in fig. 2.4.

A gas at low density is found to have no order or structure and the molecular distribution smears out to an average value.

A crystalline solid has *long range order* and the molecules are spaced evenly in a symmetrical pattern.

A liquid is characterized by *short range order*. In a liquid a typical

19

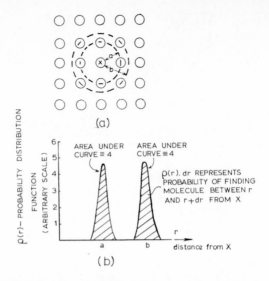

(a)

(b)

Fig. 2.3. (a) Distribution of molecules in a square two-dimensional lattice relative to a typical molecule, $X$. (b) Graphical representation of the distribution. (Note that the profiles of the curves shown in (b) vary with temperature because of thermal vibrations.)

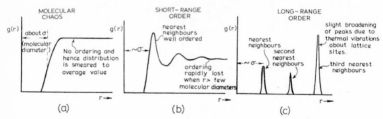

Fig. 2.4. The variation of the molecular distribution function $g(r)$ with intermolecular distance for (a) a gas (b) a liquid and (c) a solid. ($g(r) = \rho(r)/4\pi r^2$, where $\rho(r)dr$ represents the probability of finding a molecule at a distance between $r$ and $r + dr$ from $X$.)

molecule has fewer nearest neighbours than in a solid, and these are at a distance roughly comparable to the lattice spacing in a solid. The ordering in a liquid does extend beyond the nearest neighbours, but is very small beyond the second or third nearest neighbours.

We are now able to postulate simple but reasonable models to describe the properties of gases, liquids and solids. The molecules in a gas at low pressure are relatively far apart, and we know from elementary kinetic theory that they are in continuous motion, moving with a mean velocity that is proportional to the square root of the absolute temperature. The energy per molecule is nearly all kinetic and, for a monatomic gas, equal to $3kT/2$, since each molecule has three degrees of translational freedom and $kT/2$ of energy is associated with each. Collisons between molecules are rare compared with collisions between molecules and the walls of the container. If heat is removed from the gas, the average kinetic energy of the molecules decreases, and the temperature falls. Ultimately, a point is reached when molecules colliding with each other may stick together for a brief instant, and as the occurrence of such incidents reduces the average separation of the molecules, it also lowers the potential energy of the system, which, for very large intermolecular spacing may be regarded as zero (fig. 2.5).

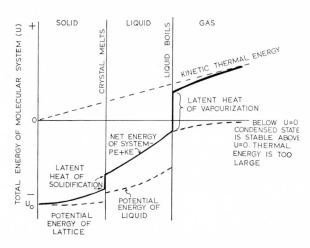

Fig. 2.5. Relative energy of a fixed number of molecules in a gas as it is condensed to a liquid and then frozen by lowering the temperature (extracting energy). Below $U=0$, the attractive forces > the disruptive influence of the thermal energy and a condensed phase is stable. (Note that this figure is not to scale and omits some features important in real systems—e.g. zero-point energy.)

The energy that is extracted from a gas as latent heat corresponds to the change in potential energy that occurs as it condenses. Since condensation takes place at constant temperature, the average kinetic energy of the system remains the same. Whereas in a gas the cohesive forces acting between molecules are small, in a liquid, because the average spacing between molecules is much reduced, the intermolecular attraction is considerably greater. Thermal motion still takes place but the movement is sluggish relative to the activity in a gas.

Freezing the liquid requires a further extraction of energy (latent heat of fusion), less than that required for condensation, and associated with the increased order and closer packing of molecules in a solid. The thermal motion of molecules in a crystal is restricted to vibrational movement about the lattice sites and is approximately equal to $3\,kT$ per molecule (see Chapter 5). Strictly speaking, even close to absolute zero the crystal still retains some vibrational energy (see Chapter 4 and § 2.4). This ' zero-point energy ' is basically due to the quantum nature of matter and arises because, according to the Heisenberg uncertainty principle, it is impossible for both the position and momentum of a particle to be precisely defined at the same instant, in this case for an atom to be completely at rest on a lattice site. For most substances, the zero-point energy is a relatively small proportion of the total lattice energy at any temperature, but for lighter atoms, in particular helium, zero-point energy is extremely important.

The forces which bind the molecules together in the liquid and solid states are ' short range forces ' which are effective only over a distance of a few molecular diameters. The resultant force acting on any one molecule can therefore be estimated by considering interactions with its nearest neighbours only, since molecules further away than a few molecular diameters will make no contribution. The resultant force acting on the representative molecule can be expressed as a ' force-pair ', acting between the molecule on the one hand and its neighbours on the other. The bulk property can then be obtained by adding up these effects for all the molecules that are present, assuming that the resultant force acting on each is the same as for the representative molecule. In this way the many-body problem of $N \approx 10^{22}$ molecules that corresponds to a reasonable-sized experimental specimen (e.g. $\sim 1\ \mu m^3$ solid) may be reduced to a summation over a large number of pair interactions.

## 2.3. *Intermolecular potentials for the inert gases*

Consider two inert gas molecules separated by a distance $r$ (fig. 2.6($a$)). Since the electron shells are full, the molecules cannot combine by forming a chemical bond, nor do they possess a permanent dipole moment (magnetic or electric) because the molecules are electrically neutral and the average distribution of charge on each molecule is symmetrical. However, F. London showed in 1930 that fluctuating dipole moments are associated with the instantaneous position of electrons in atoms and these lead to attractive forces between them.

Suppose, for example, that molecule $A$ is perturbed slightly so that the charge distribution about the nucleus becomes unsymmetrical. Then the centres of two equal and opposite charges are now separated, the whole molecule forms a temporary dipole, and will experience a torque in an electric field tending to align the electric axis with the field. The dipole moment $m$ is defined as the maximum torque in a field of unit intensity, and will be equal to $el$ where $e$ is the magnitude of the charge and $l$ the effective separation of the charge centres. The field $E$ at a point of distance $r$ from the centre of the dipole can be

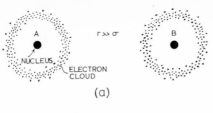

DISTORTION OF A INDUCES DISTORTION IN B

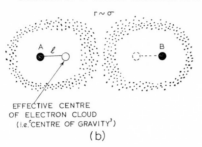

EFFECTIVE CENTRE
OF ELECTRON CLOUD
(i.e. CENTRE OF GRAVITY')

(b)

Fig. 2.6. (a) Two argon atoms separated by a distance > several atomic diameters do not interact and have time-averaged charge distributions that are symmetrical. (b) When brought closer together fluctuations in the electronic structure result in dipoles being induced in neighbours and a net dipole–dipole force ($\propto 1/r^7$) being created between molecules.

calculated by considering the combined effect of the two centres of charge distribution (i.e. nucleus and effective centre of electron clouds). It is found that providing that $r \gg l$, the field varies as $1/r^3$ and, in fact, in a direction angle $\theta$ to the magnetic axis the field may conveniently be expressed in terms of two components, $2m \cos \theta/r^3$ along the axis and $m \sin \theta/r^3$ transverse to the axis.

Now consider the effect of placing a second molecule ($B$) nearby. Because of the field arising from $A$, the charge distribution of $B$ is also shifted so that it acquires a temporary dipole moment $m'$. This is given by $m' = \alpha E$ where $\alpha$ is the polarizability (see § 8.1) and $E$ is the field due to $A$.

The two dipoles interact with each other resulting in a net attractive force. This may be estimated as follows. The force $F(r) m'$ due to $E$ is

$$F(r) = m' \, \mathrm{d}E/\mathrm{d}r$$

$$= \alpha E \, \mathrm{d}E/\mathrm{d}r$$

Because $E \propto m/r^3$,

$$F(r) \propto \alpha m/r^3 \, . \, \mathrm{d}/\mathrm{d}r \, (m/r^3)$$

$$\propto \alpha m/r^3 \, . \, 3m/r^4$$

$$\propto 3\alpha m^2/r^7$$

23

This force is sometimes called the van der Waals or dispersion force. A similar argument can be used to obtain the potential $\phi$ between the two molecular dipoles. In this case since $F(r) = -d\phi(r)/dr$, we see by integrating that the potential varies with the separation as $1/r^6$ (fig. 2.7). The important point to note is that even though the temporary dipole moment of each molecule has an average value of zero over a period of time because the charge fluctuations (effectively of either sign) occur about a neutral and symmetrical distribution, the time-averaged dipole–dipole interactions are not zero, but result in an attractive force $\propto 1/r^7$ and potential $\propto 1/r^6$.

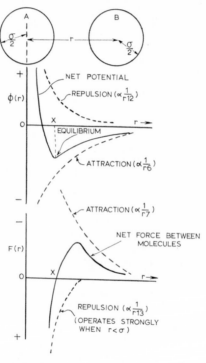

Fig. 2.7. Variation of the interatomic force and potential with separation for a pair of inert gas atoms.

What happens if $r$ is reduced so that the molecules approach each other closely? In the preceding section, the molecules were considered to be hard-spheres and therefore the repulsion became infinite for a separation less than the molecule diameter. In practice, however, as quantum mechanics shows, the electron cloud distribution that surrounds a nucleus does not finish abruptly but tails away slowly. We would therefore expect molecules to be slightly ' softer '. As the electron shells of two molecules begin to overlap, repulsive forces come into operation. These arise because of the Pauli exclusion principle (see § 1.4) and vary in similar fashion for all atoms and molecules with closed electron shells. The repulsion varies as $\exp(c/r)$, where $c$ is a constant, and therefore increases rapidly as $r$ diminishes. Although for strict accuracy the exponential term should be used in calculations, it is usually a sufficiently accurate approximation (and generally more convenient) to express the repulsive force in the form $A'r^{-n}$ where $n \approx 13$.

The cohesive and repulsive forces combine to provide the net interaction $F(r)$ between molecules (fig. 2.7). At a point $X$, for example, the two forces exactly balance. The distance $OX$ thus represents the equilibrium separation between the centres of the molecules. The interaction between the inert gas molecules can be written

$$F(r) = A'/r^n - B'/r^m$$

where $A'$ and $B'$ are positive coefficients, $n \approx 13$ and $m = 7$. The interaction may also be expressed in terms of the intermolecular potential function $\phi(r)$. Since

$$F(r) = -\frac{\mathrm{d}}{\mathrm{d}r}[\phi(r)]$$

then

$$\phi(r) = \frac{A}{r^{12}} - \frac{B}{r^6} \tag{2.1}$$

This is known as the Mie–Lennard-Jones potential in the (12,6) form.

In practice, the two molecules if in a solid crystal will not be stationary but will vibrate because of their thermal energy. At a temperature, $T$, the interatomic potential $\phi(r)$ is modified because of zero-point energy and thermal energy. As indicated in fig. 5.2 (page 60), these effectively reduce the binding energy between $A$ and $B$ from $YY$ to $Y'B$. It is often convenient to think of $B$ as lying in a potential well. At a temperature $T$, $B$ occupies an energy level $CBD$, vibrating about $B$, and between $C$ and $D$. To remove $B$ from the potential well, energy equivalent to $Y'B$ is required.

Note the convention that attractive forces are negative, and the intermolecular potential is zero at infinite separation. Equation 2.1 is often used in the form

$$\phi(r) = 4\epsilon[(\sigma/r)^{12} - (\sigma/r)^6]$$

where $A$ and $B$ have now been expressed in terms of the potential energy $\epsilon$ of two molecules at equilibrium separation ($OY$ in fig. 5.2), and the molecular diameter $\sigma$. The manner in which $\phi(r)$ varies for pairs of atoms of the different inert gases is shown in fig. 2.8.

We thus find that the interactions between pairs of inert gas molecules are spherically symmetric, short-range, and may be represented by a

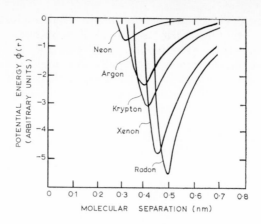

Fig. 2.8. Variation of the intermolecular potential function $\phi(r)$ with separation for pairs of inert gas molecules.

simple radial potential. The extent to which this representation is accurate will be discussed in later sections. One notable feature of van der Waals binding in molecular crystals is that it is weak compared with the other types of cohesive force that operate in dense systems when molecules are close together (see Table 2.1). Thermal properties such as specific latent heat of vaporization, and the melting temperature, provide a useful guide to the strength of the attractive forces. A high melting temperature, for example, implies that very vigorous thermal vibrations of the molecules must take place before the solid becomes unstable and melts.

| Substance | Bonding | Melting point (K) | Binding energy (J mol$^{-1}$) |
|---|---|---|---|
| argon | molecular | 84 | $7 \cdot 5 \times 10^3$ |
| sodium | metallic | 373 | $1 \cdot 1 \times 10^4$ |
| sodium chloride | ionic | 1074 | $7 \cdot 5 \times 10^5$ |
| diamond | covalent | $\sim 3800$ | $7 \cdot 1 \times 10^5$ |

Table 2.1. Properties of crystals with different types of bonding.

The atoms in an ionic crystal are held together by electrostatic forces which vary according to the inverse square law and it is possible to construct a force-diagram similar to that shown in fig. 2.7 to represent the interactions. But these cohesive forces vary as $r^{-2}$ and are therefore of longer range than the van der Waals force. In a metal crystal the ion cores are bound by the freely-moving conduction electrons, and in a covalent crystal strong electron-sharing bonds exist between atoms

26

in which the outer electron shells are each approximately half-filled. It is not possible to represent the interactions in either a metal or a covalent crystal by a simple radial potential.

## 2.4. Zero-point energy

Calculating the interactions between molecules is fundamentally a quantum mechanical problem involving all the nuclei and electrons in the system under consideration. For the heavier inert gases, the classical argument used to establish the van der Waals attractive force in the preceding section is a reasonable approximation, but for the lighter elements, quantum mechanical considerations cannot be neglected. The reason for this lies in the Heisenberg uncertainty principle, which states that if the position of a particle is known to lie within a region $\Delta x$, then its momentum may not be established to better than $\Delta p$, where $\Delta x \cdot \Delta p \approx h/2\pi$. Thus if an electron is bound to a region $\pm a/2$ in an atom, $\Delta x = a$ and the uncertainty in its momentum must be $\Delta p \gtrsim h/2\pi a$ ($h$ is Planck's constant).

In quantum mechanics, the electrons in an atom may be treated as simple harmonic oscillators. The solution to the quantum-mechanical Schrödinger wave equation shows that possible values of the energy are restricted to 'eigenstates' $E$ given by $E = (n + \frac{1}{2})h\nu$, where $\nu$ is the frequency of the oscillator and $n$ is an integer. Thus even at absolute zero temperature where there is no thermal energy and the potential energy of a crystal lattice is at the minimum, each 'oscillator' will contribute a zero point energy of $\frac{1}{2}h\nu$, ($n = 0$). An electron cannot be bound to an atom by a potential of zero energy because this would imply that the uncertainty in the momentum would also be zero, in violation of the uncertainty principle.

The energy of a typical crystal near $T = 0$ K is shown in fig. 2.9. The relative importance of zero-point energy in the different inert gases can be seen in Table 2.2. The influence is seen to decrease with increasing atomic number and becomes smaller for all elements as the temperature increases. The practical significance for helium is that because it has a relatively large zero point energy, a pressure of 2·6 MN m$^{-2}$ is required to solidify it even close to 0 K. The theoretical significance is that the properties of helium cannot be calculated by the essentially classical theories that apply quite satisfactorily to argon, krypton and xenon.

A measure of the importance of quantum effects is provided by the dimensionless parameter $\Lambda^*$ defined by

$$\Lambda^* = [h/(m\epsilon)^{1/2}]/\sigma$$

where $m$ is the mass of the atom. If $\Lambda^* \gtrsim 0.2$, quantum effects are unimportant and classical theory is applicable but as $\Lambda^*$ increases, quantum effects become increasingly important. For example, from classical theory one would expect that the volume of a crystal $V_0$ at

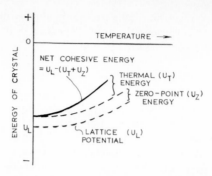

Fig. 2.9. The energy of a typical crystal near 0 K, showing the contributions of thermal and zero-point energy. At 0 K, the binding energy of the crystal is the lattice potential minus the zero-point energy. As the temperature increases, the lattice potential becomes less because the lattice expands, and the net binding energy of the crystal decreases as the atomic vibrations become larger. Also, the zero-point energy becomes a smaller fraction of the total vibrational energy as the temperature increases.

| | Lattice energy at 0 K $U_0$ (J mol$^{-1}$) | Ratio of zero point energy to lattice energy $U_z/U_0$ (expressed as a percentage) | $\epsilon$ ($10^{-23}$ J) | $\sigma$ ($10^{-10}$ m) |
|---|---|---|---|---|
| He | 50 | 392 | 14 | 2·5 |
| Ne | 1880 | 31 | 50 | 3·1 |
| Ar | 7700 | 10 | 165 | 3·8 |
| Kr | 10,800 | 5 | 227 | 4·1 |
| Xe | 16,000 | 3 | 320 | 4·4 |

Table 2.2. Table showing the relative importance of zero point energy for the inert gases, and values for the parameters $\epsilon$ and $\sigma$ in the Mie–Lennard-Jones (12, 6) potential.

$T = 0$ K would be directly proportional to $\sigma^3$. But, apart from the above equation, $\Lambda^* \propto 1/\sigma$. Thus $V_0 \propto 1/(\Lambda^*)^3$ and a plot of $V_0$ vs log $\Lambda^*$ should produce a straight line, and of $V_0/\sigma^3$ versus log $\Lambda^*$ a straight line parallel to the log $\Lambda^*$ axis. The volumes for the solidified inert gases are plotted versus log $\Lambda^*$ in fig. 2.10. It can be seen that the zero-point energy effectively swells the lattice for the two helium isotopes, so that the actual intermolecular distances are very much larger than would be expected from the potential curve.

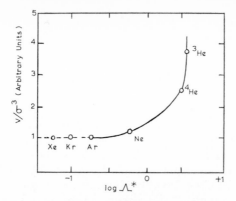

Fig. 2.10. Reduced molar volume of solidified inert gases as a function of the quantum parameter $\Lambda^*$.

## 2.5. *Phase diagrams*

All of the inert gases can be liquefied by lowering the temperature and all of the liquids, with the exception of helium, can be solidified by lowering the temperature still further. Similar changes of state may be effected by varying the pressure. Experience suggests that gas phases are stable in systems at high temperatures and low pressures, and that solid phases are to be expected at low temperatures and high pressures. The regions in which a particular phase is stable may be systematically mapped out by a series of experiments and the results represented by a phase diagram. A typical phase diagram for a substance such as argon is shown in fig. 2.11. The line $OX$ represents the sublimation curve.

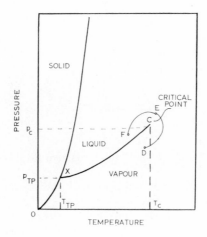

Fig. 2.11. $p$–$T$ phase diagram for argon (not to scale).

29

Any point on this line represents a state for which the solid coexists with the vapour. The line $XC$ represents the liquid–vapour coexistence curve. Pressure and temperature combinations which correspond to points along $XC$ represent states for which vapour is in equilibrium with the liquid. The relative proportions of liquid and vapour at a point depend on the molar volume (i.e. the density) of the substance.

The properties of the vapour and liquid tend to converge along $XC$, until at the critical point $C$ they become identical. Whereas crossing the line $XC$ is accompanied by evolution or absorption of latent heat and by discontinuity in physical properties such as density and refractive index, at temperatures above the critical point $C$ ($T_c$) the distinction between a liquid and a gas is lost. Indeed, by following the thermo-dynamic path $DEF$, it is possible to change from a gas to a liquid without apparent discontinuity. The striking phenomena associated with the critical region are discussed in Chapter 7. The melting curve, separat-ing the liquid and solid regions does not appear to have a critical point. Experiments on helium under very high pressures suggest that the properties of the liquid and the solid diverge rather than converge, and it is unlikely therefore that a solid–liquid critical point exists.

The $p$–$T$ phase diagram for $^4$He is quite different from those of the other inert gases, because it does not have a triple point (fig. 2.12).

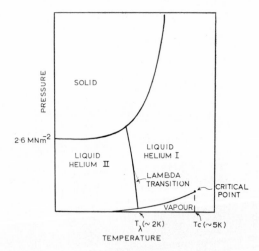

Fig. 2.12.    $p$–$T$ phase diagram for $^4$He.

The liquid can remain in equilibrium with the vapour down to 0 K and to solidify the liquid a pressure in excess of $2 \cdot 6$ MN m$^{-2}$ must be applied. This is due to the zero point energy, already discussed in the preceding section. Another feature of the phase diagram is the $\lambda$-line at which there is a transition from helium I to helium II. Helium

II exhibits some very unusual properties which have been briefly summarized in § 1.5.

The phase diagram of $^3$He is somewhat similar to that of $^4$He, but $^3$He does not have a $\lambda$ transition.

One can draw phase diagrams using other thermodynamic variables (for example, $p$ and $V$) and some of these will be used in later sections of this book. Two points should be made here, however. The first is that phase diagrams should really be drawn in three dimensions with, for example, $p$, $V$ and $T$ as the three axes. Phase boundaries in three dimensions are surfaces and those shown in fig. 2.11 are in fact projections of these surfaces onto the $p$–$T$ plane. The second point is that although $p$, $V$ and $T$ are the thermodynamic coordinates most commonly used to specify the thermal state of a substance, they are by no means the most useful, because they give no indication of the energy state of a system, i.e. whether it is in equilibrium. There are other thermodynamic coordinates that can be used for example, $G$, the Gibbs free energy or $F$, the Helmholtz free energy (see Appendix). It is quite in order to specify the state of a system by $G$, $V$ and $T$ rather than $p$, $V$ and $T$. Not only is this useful because $G$ is a measure of the energy of the system (the state corresponding to the lowest possible $G$ value is the equilibrium state), but also $p$ may be derived from $G$, $V$ and $T$. Phase diagrams may be drawn with $G$, $V$ and $T$ as the axes and although these may be unfamiliar they are very useful. For example, one can draw contours of constant $G_S$ within the solid region. Similar surfaces could be drawn within the liquid ($G_L$). These surfaces intersect in a line when $G_L = G_S$ (the melting curve). Similarly the line of interesection $G_L = G_V$ is the vapourization curve, and $G_S = G_V$ is the sublimation curve. These three lines meet at a point where $G_S = G_L = G_V$, i.e. the triple point.

# CHAPTER 3

## gases

### 3.1. *Ideal gases*

AN ideal gas consists of molecules of finite mass but negligible volume, moving randomly, and colliding elastically with the walls of the container. It is assumed that intermolecular forces are negligible. The properties of real gases approach those of ideal gases in the limit of low pressure and high temperature, although the equation of state for 1 mole of an ideal gas, $pV = RT$, may be used to describe the properties of gases at atmospheric pressure and room temperature sufficiently accurately for many purposes.

According to kinetic theory, a gas exerts pressure because of the impacts between the molecules and the walls of the container. If the container is isolated from its surroundings, the gas pressure reaches a certain value, the equilibrium pressure, which depends on the volume, temperature, and amount of gas. The pressure is independent of time, and therefore the collisions must be elastic, since this implies that there is no loss of kinetic energy. The average kinetic energy per molecule ($\bar{\epsilon}$) of the molecules in equilibrium is a function only of the absolute temperature, and

$$\bar{\epsilon} \propto T$$

Suppose that at a given instant the velocities of all the $N$ molecules in the gas could be measured. The results could be represented graphically as follows. Divide the velocity range into a number of intervals. The number of molecules with velocities falling in each interval can be counted and the totals represented by a histogram as shown in fig. 3.1($a$). The area under each section of the histogram represents the fraction of the measurements falling within this interval and the ordinate is the probability density $f(v)$. The significance of the probability density is that $N \cdot f(v) \cdot \Delta v$. represents the number of molecules with velocities that lie between $v$ and $v + \Delta v$. If the total number of molecules is large, the interval size may be reduced but a reasonable number of velocities will still fall into each interval. As $N$ tends to infinity, the chosen intervals may be reduced further until the distribution becomes the continuous curve shown in fig. 3.1($b$). In this case, the probability of a particular measurement lying in the interval $v$ to $v + dv$ is $f(v) \cdot dv$ and the total number of molecules with velocities in this interval is $N \cdot f(v) \cdot dv$.

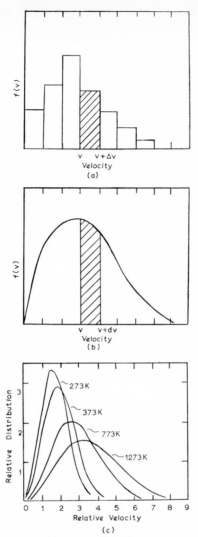

Fig. 3.1. Relative distribution of molecular velocities represented as (a) histogram, (b) continuous curve, (c) distribution at different temperatures according to the Maxwell–Boltzmann law.

The shape of a probability density curve depends on the nature of the random process being measured. In the case of the velocity distribution in a gas, the curve is given by the Maxwell–Boltzmann distribution function $p(v)$, where

$$p(v)\,\mathrm{d}v = 4\pi v^2 \left(\frac{m}{2\pi kT}\right)^{3/2} \exp\left(-\frac{mv^2}{2kT}\right)\mathrm{d}v$$

represents the fraction of molecules with velocities that lie in the range $v$ to $v+\mathrm{d}v$. The dependence of the distribution on temperature is shown in fig. 3.1($c$).

The contribution of the molecules to the bulk gas properties may be estimated as follows. Consider a small volume $\Delta V$ of a monatomic gas containing $n$ molecules per unit volume (fig. 3.2). If we examine the distribution of the molecular velocities, we find that the probability of finding a velocity in the range $v$ to $v+\mathrm{d}v$ without taking direction into account is

$$f(v)\ \mathrm{d}v = 4\pi v^2 p(v)\ \mathrm{d}v$$

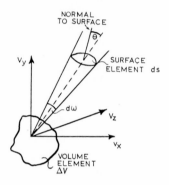

Fig. 3.2.  Figure used to calculate the molecular flow from a volume element $\Delta V$ across a surface d$s$ in unit time.

The average number of molecules with velocities that lie in the range $v$ to $v+\mathrm{d}v$ that are also travelling in a direction specified by the solid angle d$\omega$ is

$$n\Delta V p(v)\ \mathrm{d}v\ \frac{\mathrm{d}\omega}{4\pi}.$$

Each molecule that crosses the surface area $\Delta s$ contributes 1 to the number flow, $mv\cos\theta$ to the flow of momentum perpendicular to $\Delta s$ and $\frac{1}{2}mv^2$ to the energy flow. The contribution to the flow per time $\Delta t$ from the molecules in $\Delta V$ with velocities lying between $v$ and $v+\mathrm{d}v$ is therefore

$$\text{number flow }(J_n) = nv\cos\theta\Delta t\ \Delta s\ \Delta V\ .\ p(v)\ \mathrm{d}v\ \frac{\Delta\omega}{4\pi}\times 1$$

$$\text{momentum flow }(J_p) = nv\cos\theta\Delta t\ \Delta s\ \Delta V\ .\ p(v)\ \mathrm{d}v\ \frac{\Delta\omega}{4\pi}\times mv\cos\theta$$

$$\text{energy flow }(J_e) = nv\cos\theta\Delta t\ \Delta s\ \Delta V\ .\ p(v)\ \mathrm{d}v\ \frac{\Delta\omega}{4\pi}\times\tfrac{1}{2}mv^2$$

34

The total flow per unit area per unit time may be calculated by integrating the above expressions over velocity space, i.e. for all velocities and directions. The results are

$$J_n = \frac{1}{4}n \int v p(v) \mathrm{d}v = \frac{1}{4}n\bar{v} = \frac{n}{\sqrt{2\pi}} \left(\frac{kT}{m}\right)^{1/2}$$

$$J_p = \frac{1}{6}nm \int v^2 p(v)\,\mathrm{d}v = \frac{1}{6}nm\overline{v^2} = \frac{1}{2}nkT$$

and

$$J_e = \frac{1}{8}nm \int v^3 p(v)\,\mathrm{d}v = \frac{1}{8}nm\overline{v^3} = \sqrt{\frac{2}{\pi}}\, nm \left(\frac{kT}{m}\right)^{3/2}$$

Note that $J_p$ represents the momentum per unit area per unit time transferred perpendicular to the area and in one direction only. If there is reflection, i.e. the molecules rebound elastically from the walls of a container, then there is an additional negative momentum in the opposite direction which must be taken into account. The *total* flow of momentum is thus $nkT$.

The average kinetic energy per molecule is $\frac{1}{2}m\,\overline{c^2} = 3kT/2 = \bar{\epsilon}$, so that the average translational kinetic energy for one mole of gas at temperature $T$ is $3N_A\bar{\epsilon}/2 = 3RT/2$, where $N_A$ is Avogadro's number and $R$ is the universal gas constant. Since $R \approx 8.4$ J mol$^{-1}$ K$^{-1}$, the molar translational kinetic energy of an ideal gas at room temperature ($\sim 300$ K) is about $3.8$ kJ mol$^{-1}$.

Now let us look at some of the thermal properties of an ideal gas. The molar heat capacity at constant volume is defined by

$$C_v = \left(\frac{\partial U}{\partial T}\right)_V = 3R/2 \approx 12.6 \text{ J mol}^{-1} \text{ K}^{-1}$$

If the gas was allowed to expand when heated in such a way as to keep the pressure constant, the gas must absorb heat in addition to $C_v$ equivalent to the work done $= p\mathrm{d}V$. For one mole of gas heated through 1 K, this is $R(T+1) - RT = R$, therefore the molar heat capacity at constant pressure $C_p$ is related to $C_v$ by

$$C_p - C_v = R$$

and the ratio

$$C_p/C_v = \gamma = 5/3.$$

Note that the above discussion applies to monatomic molecules, e.g. the inert gases, which have 3 degrees of translational freedom. Diatomic molecules may vibrate along their axes and non-linear polyatomic molecules are able to both vibrate and rotate. The effect of these additional modes is to increase the total possible kinetic energy.

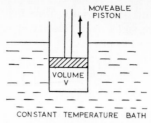

Fig. 3.3.   Isothermal compression or expansion of an ideal gas.

The work done in expanding or compressing a mole of gas may be calculated by considering the gas to be held in a cylinder fitted with a moveable piston (fig. 3.3).   If the cylinder is kept at a constant temperature by placing it in a water bath, and the piston is moved slowly, the change is isothermal and the work done is the product of the force and the distance through which it acts.

The work done in changing the volume from $V_1$ to $V_2$ is

$$\int_{V_1}^{V_2} -p\,\mathrm{d}V = -RT \int_{V_1}^{V_2} \frac{\mathrm{d}V}{V} = RT \ln (V_1/V_2)$$

If, however, the cylinder is well lagged and the piston is moved rapidly, the change is adiabatic and is accompanied by a rise in temperature.   Energy equivalent to the work carried out during the compression is transferred to the kinetic energy of the molecules.   Instead of Boyle's law, we have:

$$(p_2/p_1) = (V_1/V_2)^\gamma,$$

and instead of Charles' law:

$$(T_2/T_1) = (p_2/p_1)^{R/C_p}$$

There is one other property of an ideal gas that should be noted. It is useful in thermodynamics to define the enthalpy $H$ of a system as

$$H = U + pV$$

where $U$ is the internal energy.

When a gas is 'throttled', i.e. forced under a pressure gradient through a small hole adiabatically (fig. 3.4), the enthalpy change is zero, and it can be shown that under these conditions a temperature change $\Delta T$ occurs in the gas, given by

$$\left(\frac{\Delta T}{\Delta p}\right) = \frac{1}{C_p}\left[T\left(\frac{\partial V}{\partial T}\right)_p - V\right] \tag{3.1}$$

$[(\partial V/\partial T)_p]$ denotes partial differentiation: i.e. one differentiates $V$ with respect to $T$, assuming that $p$ is a constant].

36

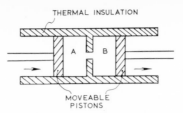

Fig. 3.4. A gas is 'throttled' by passing it from chamber $A$ to chamber $B$ through a small hole under a pressure gradient, generated by movement of the two pistons.

Now for one mole of an ideal gas

$$pV = RT,$$

or

$$V = RT/p$$

Therefore

$$\left(\frac{\partial V}{\partial T}\right)_p = R/p$$

and

$$\left(\frac{\Delta T}{\Delta p}\right) = \frac{1}{C_p}\left(\frac{RT}{p} - V\right) = 0$$

No temperature change would therefore be observed in an ideal gas. Throttling, which is an important method for cooling gases and is often used as a stage in a helium liquefier, depends for its success on the deviations of real gases from ideal gas behaviour. This will be discussed in the next section.

### 3.2. *Real gases*

When the temperature of a gas is lowered, or it is compressed, the molecules no longer occupy a negligible volume compared with the volume of the gas, and attractive forces between molecules become significant. The deviations from the ideal gas laws become very large at high pressures, even for the simple inert gas molecules (fig. 3.5).

The best known simple model for real gas is represented by the van der Waals equation

$$(p + a/V^2)(V - b) = RT \tag{3.2}$$

Because the molecules have finite volume, the space in which they are free to move is less than the volume of the container by an amount $b$ per mole. The pressure in a real gas is less than that of an ideal gas because of the attraction between molecules and since binary collisions predominate, the effect is proportional to $1/V^2$. The constant $a$ is a measure of the strength of the attractive force between a pair of molecules.

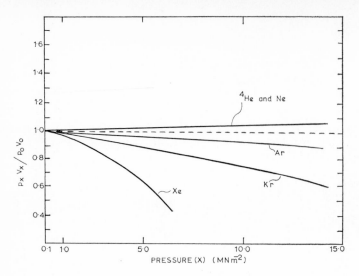

Fig. 3.5. Variation of the compressibility factor of the inert gases at 294 K with pressure. ($p_x V_x$ is $pV$ value at pressure $X$. $p_0 V_0$ is $pV$ value at 0·1 MN m⁻².)

The van der Waals equation is remarkable since it provides a reasonable qualitative description of a great many physical properties associated with real gases and liquids. For this reason it is worth examining in some detail. First of all, compare the van der Waals equation written in the form

$$p + a/V^2 = RT/(V-b) \qquad (3.3)$$

with the purely thermodynamic equation of state, derivable from general principles,

$$p + (\partial U/\partial V)_T = T(\partial p/\partial T)_V \qquad (3.4)$$

The term $(\partial U/\partial V)_T$ represents the change produced in the internal energy ($U$) of a system when the volume is altered under constant temperature conditions. It is a measure of the cohesion in the fluid. The left hand sides of equations (3.3) and (3.4) are therefore similar, because they both represent the forces that tend to oppose the fluid expanding—the *external pressure* $p$ and the *internal pressure* $(\partial U/\partial V)_T$ or $a/V^2$. In the same way, the term $(\partial p/\partial T)_V$ which is the rate at which the pressure increases with temperature when the volume is held constant, is equivalent to $RT/(V-b)$. Both represent the repulsive forces in the fluid—the tendency of the fluid to expand.

The van der Waals isotherms for argon are shown in fig. 3.6. Equation (3.2) may be rearranged into the form:

$$V^3 - (b + RT/p)V^2 + (a/p)V - ab/p = 0$$

38

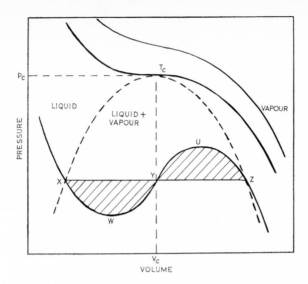

Fig. 3.6.  Van der Waals isotherms for argon (not to scale).

This is a cubic equation in $V$ and within certain limits the solution has three real roots, e.g. $X$, $Y$ and $Z$ in fig. 3.6. The behaviour of the isotherms is qualitatively correct. As $(T_c - T)$ increases, $V \to b$, and at large volume the isotherms tend to take on the shape of the rectangular hyperbolas predicted by the ideal gas law. In the region enclosed by the dashed line there is a non-equilibrium situation in which two phases coexist. The van der Waals equation by itself is not sufficient to define this region, and the Maxwell equal area rule is generally invoked for this purpose. Consider the region $X$, $Y$, $Z$. According to the equal area rule, a line $XYZ$ is drawn such that the area $XWY$ is equal to the area $YUZ$, when the points $X$ and $Z$ should represent the volumes of the liquid and vapour in equilibrium at that temperature and pressure. As $T \to T_c$, $XZ$ decreases in length, and vanishes entirely when $T = T_c$. At the critical point, the critical isotherm has a horizontal tangent $(\partial p / \partial V)_{T_c} = 0$ and also a point of inflection $(\partial^2 p / \partial V^2)_{T_c} = 0$. The striking and anomalous physical phenomena associated with the critical point are discussed in Chapter 7.

The section of isotherm that lies between $W$ and $U$ represents a situation that is mechanically impossible since it implies that an increase in pressure produces an increase in volume. However, the sections $ZU$ and $XW$ of the isotherm are physically realisable in many cases, representing, respectively, metastable conditions in which the pressure of the vapour may be raised, beyond the point at which condensation would normally occur without liquid forming, and lowered in the liquid beyond the point at which evaporation or boiling should occur, without vapour appearing. These phenomena may be observed in extremely pure argon. At low temperatures, the van der Waals isotherms pass below the volume axis. This situation is not quite so improbable as it may appear at first sight since it is possible to obtain a 'negative pressure' in a liquid. For example, if liquid argon is formed in a thick-walled glass bulb fitted with a valve (fig. 3.7), and the valve is then closed, a slight heating of the bulb will cause the residual vapour to disappear and the liquid to fill the entire volume. Subsequent cooling can then take place to several degrees below the temperature at which the bubble disappeared, without it reappearing, but a sharp tap on the glass produces a sudden surge of small bubbles within the liquid. Negative pressures that correspond to $\sim -1$ MNm$^{-2}$ or even higher can be obtained by this method.

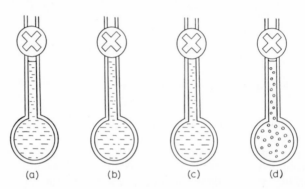

Fig. 3.7. Stages in the formation of 'negative pressure' within liquid argon. (a) Liquid argon is isolated in a glass bulb. (b) Residual vapour disappears at temperature $T_1$ upon slight heating of the bulb. (c) Slow cooling below $T_1$ produces state of 'negative pressure' within liquid. (d) At a temperature $T_2$ ($< T_1$) bubbles of vapour suddenly appear.

Before leaving the van der Waals equation, it is worth while using it to estimate the relative importance of kinetic and potential energy under various conditions. This may be done with the help of equation (3.4). We have already seen that $(\partial U/\partial V)_T$ is equivalent to $a/V^2$, therefore the internal energy $U$ may be estimated by integrating $a/V^2$ along an isothermal, i.e.

$$U = -a/V + \alpha(T)$$

The integration constant $\alpha(T)$ may be evaluated by recognizing that the behaviour of argon tends to that of an ideal gas as the volume tends to infinity.

Thus

$$\text{Limit}_{V \to \infty} \; U = \alpha(T) = 3RT/2$$

and so

$$U = -a/V + 3RT/2 \tag{3.5}$$

40

| | $T$ (K) | $V$ ($10^{-3}$ m$^3$) | $U_{pot}$ (J) | $U_{kin}$ (J) | $U_{total}$ (J) |
|---|---|---|---|---|---|
| Gas | 273 | 22·4 | −6 | +3400 | +3394 |
| Critical fluid | 150·7 | 0·075 | −1800 | ∼1850 | ∼50 |
| Vapour at normal B.P. | 87·3 | 6·8 | −20 | +1100 | −1080 |
| Liquid at normal B.P. | 87·3 | 0·029 | −4800 | +1100 | −3700 |

Table 3.1. Relative contributions of kinetic energy and potential energy to the total energy of 1 mole of argon, calculated for a van der Waals fluid. ($U_{pot} = -a/V$ and $U_{kin} = 3RT/2$.)

Values of $-a/V$ and $3RT/2$ calculated for argon are given in Table 3.1. The values are in error by a factor of up to 100% in some cases. Other quantitative predictions of the van der Waals equation have also been shown to be incorrect, for example $RT_c/P_cV_c = 2·67$, compared with measured values of $\sim 3·0$ for argon, krypton and xenon. However, the qualitative picture provided by this simple semi-empirical equation is quite remarkable. Many other equations of state have been proposed to account for the properties of fluids, some of which contain a large number of adjustable parameters. However useful these may be for practical purposes, they add very little to the basic knowledge of the subject and will not be discussed here.

### 3.3. *Virial equations*

A convenient method for expressing the deviations of real gases from the ideal gas law $pV = RT$ is to expand the equation of state in terms of either volume or pressure

$$pV/RT = 1 + B(T)/V + C(T)/V^2 + D(T)/V^3$$

$$pV/RT = 1 + B'(T)p + C'(T)p^2 + D'(T)p^3 \qquad (3.6)$$

where $B(T)$, $C(T)$ etc. are the second, third and higher coefficients. The coefficients in the two series are of course related, for example

$$B' = B/RT \quad \text{and} \quad C' = (C - B^2)/(RT)^2$$

Representation in the virial form is convenient because it is possible to calculate the coefficients using statistical mechanics. It is also possible to relate the terms to experimentally observed quantities. For example the coefficients $B(T)$ and $C(T)$ represent the effects of interactions involving two and three molecules, respectively. The im-

41

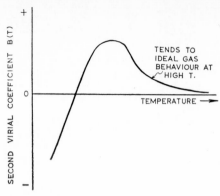

Fig. 3.8. Variation of second virial coefficient $B(T)$ of argon with temperature.

portance of the terms diminishes rapidly and therefore interest has centred around the first few coefficients. In particular, $B(T)$ has been systematically calculated for slightly imperfect gases, assuming a wide range of force laws. It is found (fig. 3.8) that $B(T)$ is negative at low temperatures, becomes positive at higher temperatures, passes through a maximum and then decreases to zero.

The range of validity of a series expansion such as is given in equation (3.6) depends on the convergence of the series. At low and moderate densities the equation may be made as accurate as required by including a sufficiently large number of terms. At the higher densities corresponding to the liquid phase however, the series diverges and alternative methods have to be employed to describe the properties.

Let us examine in greater detail how $B(T)$ may be determined from experimental data. For a slightly imperfect gas, a technique known as the Mayer Cluster method may be used to establish the virial coefficients. The second coefficient is given by

$$B(T) = -2\pi N_A \int_0^\infty [\exp -(\phi(r)/kT) - 1] r^2 \, dr$$

where $\phi(r)$ is the interatomic potential between two atoms distance $r$ apart (see § 2.3). Since $\phi(r)$ may be written in terms of $\epsilon$ and $\sigma$, the well depth and nearest approach of atoms in the Mie–Lennard–Jones potential, $B(T)$ may also be expressed in terms of $\epsilon$ and $\sigma$. Experimental values for $\epsilon$ and $\sigma$ can be obtained from a throttling experiment similar to the one described in § 3.1. This time, however, instead of the quantity $(\Delta T/\Delta p) = 0$, as it is for an ideal gas, $(\Delta T/\Delta p)$ may be either positive or negative depending on the temperature. This may be seen by expressing equation (3.1) in the form:

$$(\Delta T/\Delta p) = \frac{1}{C_p} \left\{ \left( \frac{\partial U}{\partial p} \right)_T + \left[ \frac{\partial (pV)}{\partial p} \right]_T \right\}$$

42

The term $(\partial U/\partial p)_T$ represents the departure of the gas from Joules' law ($U$ depends only on $T$), and $[\partial(pV)/\partial p]_T$ represents the deviation from Boyles' law ($pV = $ constant). $(\partial U/\partial p)_T$ is always negative because of the work done in overcoming the attractive forces between molecules when the volume is expanded. The deviations from Boyles' law are negative at low pressures and positive at high pressures. By a careful analysis of the observed variation of ($\Delta T/\Delta p$) with pressure and temperature, values of $\epsilon$ and $\sigma$ may be extracted that give the best fit to the data.

This is not the only method available for estimating the parameters $\epsilon$ and $\sigma$. For example, another value for $\sigma$ can be obtained from viscosity measurements. Consider a molecule moving through a gas (fig. 3.9). The mean distance that it travels between collisions ($\lambda$)

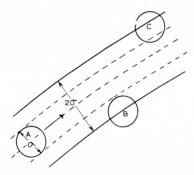

Fig. 3.9. Molecule $A$ collides with all other molecules whose centres lie within a distance $\sigma$ from the path traced out by the centre of $A$. Thus it just misses $B$ but collides with $C$.

depends on the size and density of the molecules in the gas. A molecule $A$ collides with any other molecule in its path whose centre lies less than $\sigma$ from the line of flight. Between collisions, therefore, no other molecule is encountered within an imaginary cylinder of cross section $\pi\sigma^2$ and length $\lambda$. After $n$ collisions it will have traced out a volume $\pi n \sigma^2 \lambda \approx 1$. (There are $n$ molecules per unit volume of gas.) Therefore

$$\lambda = 1/(\sqrt{2}\pi n \sigma^2)$$

(The factor $\sqrt{2}$ is introduced to take account of momentum exchange between colliding molecules.) Elementary kinetic theory gives as the viscosity $\eta$ of a gas

$$\eta = \frac{1}{3} nm\, \bar{v}\lambda$$

so that

$$\eta = \frac{1}{3} m\, \bar{v}/(\sqrt{2}\pi\sigma^2)$$

43

The values of $\sigma$ and $\epsilon$ obtained by these different methods differ slightly, but agreement for the monatomic inert gases is on the whole quite good.

## 3.4. Conclusions

Attempts to treat a dense gas as a slightly imperfect ideal gas are, as we have seen, doomed to failure. From a statistical mechanical viewpoint it is more realistic to place substances in the categories low density gas, fluid (dense gas and liquid) and solid, rather than the more conventional gas, liquid and solid. Although the properties of a slightly imperfect gas may be described using series methods and approximations, at even moderate densities the approach fails. As will be seen in Chapter 6, it is only comparatively recently that much progress has been made towards solving the problem of a dense fluid or liquid.

# CHAPTER 4

## crystal structure and growth

### 4.1. *Structure of the solidified inert gases*

FOR some years it has been recognized that, solidified, the inert gases are very useful materials for studying the properties of the solid state. The crystals are close-packed in structure i.e., there is minimum free space between the atoms. The intermolecular cohesive forces are of the van der Waals dispersion type, are central, and can be represented to a good approximation by simple radial potentials. And the effects of free electrons do not have to be taken into consideration. These and other factors help to simplify the formulation of the theory and to make the calculations possible. This chapter will deal chiefly with the structure and growth of solid specimens.

What is the stable structure of an inert gas crystal? Because the molecules are spherically symmetrical, one would certainly expect them to form a close-packed lattice. It has been proved by M. Born that for atoms which interact with a potential of the form $\phi(r) = A/r^n - B/r^m$, provided that $n > m$ and $m \geqslant 5$, only two lattice structures are mechanically stable—the close-packed (face centred) cubic lattice and the hexagonal close-packed lattice (fig. 4.1). Lattices that are more loosely packed (for example body-centred cubic) or of lower symmetry (such as tetragonal) would not be expected to be formed with identical spherical atoms. Curiously enough, although most theoretical calculations indicate that the hexagonal close-packed should be the favoured one, experiment shows that, except in the case of solid helium, only the face-centred cubic structure is observed.

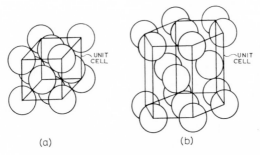

Fig. 4.1. (*a*) Face-centred cubic and (*b*) hexagonal close-packed distribution of spherical molecules.

45

Let us examine the difference between a face-centred cubic lattice and a hexagonal close-packed lattice. Starting with a typical molecule $A$, the two systems may be constructed as follows. First of all six other identical molecules may be placed in contact with $A$ and in the same plane. A close-packed structure repeats this pattern in three dimensions. However, when one carries this out in practice it is found that the layers may be fitted together in two distinct ways. In fig. 4.2(a) it is seen that there are six possible sites available on which a molecule could be placed on top of the original layer so that it is in a hollow (potential minimum) and also is in contact with $A$. But once it is placed in position, as in fig. 4.2(a), only two of the remaining sites may be used by the other molecules. Molecules may be added below the original layer in a similar fashion. The molecule $A$ thus ends up having twelve neighbours in contact—six in the same plane, plus three above and three below. We say that the *co-ordination number* is twelve.

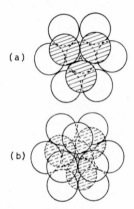

(a)

(b)

Fig. 4.2. Alternative methods for three-dimensional close-packing of spherical molecules. (a) Hexagonal close packed. (b) Face-centred cubic (the posterior layer is shaded).

A different arrangement may be obtained by keeping the original layer and the bottom layer fixed but moving the upper molecules to the positions shown in fig. 4.2(b). In fig. 4.2(a) the centres of the molecules in the upper layer are vertically above those in the bottom layer. They form a lattice with hexagonal symmetry about an axis through $A$, normal to the figure. In fig. 4.2(b) the centres of the spheres in the top layer lie above the spaces between the spheres in the bottom layer. This arrangement has cubic symmetry and corresponds to a face-centred cubic lattice. These are the only two possible ways of constructing a lattice with a co-ordination number of twelve. The atoms in all other possible lattices are packed less closely and have smaller co-ordination numbers.

The equilibrium crystal structure is a function of the external conditions, the temperature and pressure. It is that configuration for which the Gibbs free energy $G = U + pV - TS$ is a minimum (see Appendix). At 0 K the lattice energy per mole is

$$U_0 = U_Z + U_L = U_Z + \tfrac{1}{2} N_A \sum_{ij} \phi(r_{ij}) \qquad (4.1)$$

where $U_Z$ is the zero-point vibrational energy (see § 2.4), and $U_L$ is the potential energy, $\phi(r_{ij})$, between each pair of atoms within the lattice, summed over all the lattice. (The factor $\tfrac{1}{2}$ is included so that atoms are not counted twice in the summation.) If the zero-point energy is small compared with the lattice potential, then $G = U_0 \approx U_L$ and the equilibrium structure is the one for which $U_L$ is a minimum.

Estimates of the lattice energy may be made by determining the molar heat of sublimation at 0 K. To a good approximation this should represent the energy required to separate all the molecules to infinity, although in practice it assumes that during the process of sublimation, the molecules acquire negligible kinetic energy. Neglecting zero-point energy and considering the twelve nearest neighbours only, breaking all the bonds in one mole of the solid requires an energy

$$U_L = \tfrac{1}{2} N_A \cdot 12 \cdot \epsilon = 6 N_A \epsilon$$

where $\epsilon$ is the depth of the intermolecular potential well (see § 2.3). If second nearest neighbours also are taken into consideration, $U_L = 6 \cdot 4 N_A \epsilon$. Table 4.1 shows that estimates of $U_L$ based on experimental data are in very fair agreement with the above predictions.

| | $\epsilon$ $(10^{-23}$ J) | $U_L$ (J mol$^{-1}$) | |
|---|---|---|---|
| | | Calculated | Observed |
| helium | 14 | 505 | 50 |
| neon | 50 | 1 800 | 1 880 |
| argon | 165 | 5 950 | 7 700 |
| krypton | 227 | 8 200 | 10 800 |
| xenon | 320 | 11 550 | 16 000 |

Table 4.1. Comparison of the lattice energy $U_L$ calculated from $U_L = 6 N_A \epsilon$ with the observed heat of sublimation extrapolated to 0 K.

Calculation of the energy $U_L$ of a lattice structure at 0 K is relatively straightforward for the solidified inert gases. Consider the face-centred cubic structure of fig. 4.3. The potential energy between any pair of molecules separated by a distance $r$ is $\phi(r) = A/r^{12} - B/r^6$ in the Mie–Lennard-Jones form. Each atom has twelve nearest neighbours

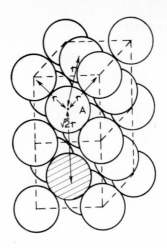

Fig. 4.3. Face-centred cubic structure, showing the positions of some of the nearest (○) and second nearest neighbours (◉) from molecule $A$.

at a separation of $r$, six second-nearest neighbours at a distance $\sqrt{2}\,r$ and twenty-four third-nearest neighbours at a distance $\sqrt{3}\,r$. The total attractive part of the interatomic potential is therefore

$$-\left[\frac{12B}{r^6}+\frac{6B}{(\sqrt{2}\,r)^6}+\frac{24B}{(\sqrt{3}\,r)^6}+\ldots\right]\approx-\frac{12\cdot8B}{r^6} \qquad (4.3)$$

The repulsive forces may also be grouped together in a single term so that the net lattice energy becomes

$$\phi(r)=\frac{A}{r^{12}}-\frac{12\cdot8B}{r^6} \qquad (4.2)$$

At the equilibrium separation $r=r_0$, $(\partial\phi(r)/\partial r)=0$ and the lattice potential $U_L=\frac{1}{2}N_A\phi(r)$ is a minimum. Differentiating $U_L$ with respect to $r$, we find that $A=6\cdot4r_0^6B$, hence

$$U_L=6\cdot4N_AB\left[\frac{r_0^6}{2r^{12}}-\frac{1}{r^6}\right] \qquad (4.3)$$

At the equilibrium separation therefore,

$$U_L=-3\cdot2N_AB/r_0^6 \qquad (4.4)$$

A similar calculation may be carried out for the hexagonal close-packed structure, using the appropriate co-ordination numbers and intermolecular spacings. At $0\,\mathrm{K}$ the hexagonal close-packed system is found to have a free energy that is lower than that for the face-centred cubic system by $0\cdot01\%$. The reason for the smallness of the difference

| | First nearest neighbours | | Second nearest neighbours | | Third nearest neighbours | |
|---|---|---|---|---|---|---|
| | number | distance | number | distance | number | distance |
| f.c.c. | 12 | $r$ | 6 | $\sqrt{2}\,r$ | 24 | $(3)^{\frac{1}{2}}r$ |
| h.c.p. | 12 | $r$ | 6 | $\sqrt{2}\,r$ | 2 | $(8/3)^{\frac{1}{2}}r$ |

Table 4.2. Comparison of neighbours in face-centred cubic (f.c.c.) and hexa-gonal close-packed (h.c.p.) systems. Although the first and second co-ordination numbers are identical, the actual distribution of molecules in the two lattices is different ($r$ is approximately equal to the molecular diameter).

is seen by reference to Table 4.2. It is only at third nearest neighbour distances that differences between the two lattices begin to appear. It is also possible to estimate the effect of pressure on the two lattices at 0 K. In fact it is found that the calculated energy difference diminishes with increasing pressure until about 10 GN m⁻², where the free energy of the cubic structure becomes the lower.

These calculations have all been carried out for 0 K. To compute the stable structure at $T > 0$ K it is necessary to evaluate the temperature dependence of the Gibbs free energy

$$\left(\frac{\partial G}{\partial T}\right)_p = -\int C_p \left(\frac{\mathrm{d}T}{T}\right) \propto \frac{1}{\Theta_D^3}$$

where $C_p$ is the molar heat capacity at constant pressure and $\Theta_D$ is a characteristic thermal parameter, defined in terms of the maximum vibration frequency $\nu_D$ of atomic oscillators within the crystal ($\Theta_D = h\nu_D/k$), and called the Debye temperature (see §5.1). It is possible that if $\Theta_D$ for a hexagonal close-packed lattice is greater than that of a cubic close-packed lattice, then a phase transition from f.c.c. to h.c.p. might be observed at a certain temperature above which $G_{\text{f.c.c.}} > G_{\text{h.c.p.}}$. So far, experiments down to 4.2 K on the heavier inert gases indicated that only the cubic structure is stable in the pure solids. However, studies at lower temperatures might reveal such a transition.

Calculations of the free energy as a function of temperature also suggest that hexagonal close-packed should be the stable structure. Again, the principal difference in energy between the two lattices arises because of the difference in number and position of the third nearest neighbours.

It should be noted, however, that although the first and second co-ordination numbers are the same for the two lattices, the actual positions of molecules in the two lattices are different, so that if the

49

dipole–dipole two-body forces are *not* strictly radial, but are slightly directional, or are modified by the angular distribution of other molecules, then a difference in the lattice sums may exist, even over nearest neighbours. Another possibility that might account for the difference is that the pattern of nearest neighbours in a hexagonal close-packed lattice is such that groups of four molecules may form 'octupoles', and the repulsion between neighbouring octupoles may be sufficient to decrease the stability by the appropriate amount. The cubic system may be made stable at all temperatures if 'many-body' forces are invoked, or if the pair-potential is modified sufficiently. The problem is still by no means entirely resolved.

## 4.2. *Crystal growth*

In the condensed state the inert gases form colourless liquids and, under suitable conditions, freeze into compact transparent solids. Often the solid is sufficiently clear to give the misleading impression that it consists of a defect-free single crystal. However, several X-ray studies have shown that solid argon when formed under normal conditions consists of a large number of polycrystals of grain size $\sim 10^{-4}$ m in diameter. Most of the work so far has been done on polycrystalline samples and it is only relatively recently that large single crystals have been produced. Some properties, for example, the refractive index, presumably will not differ much whether the specimen is polycrystalline or whether it is a single crystal (see Chapter 8). However, other properties, including mechanical strength and thermal conductivity, are extremely sensitive to the presence of structural defects in the solid.

Most experiments to date have been carried out on polycrystalline samples because it has proved to be extremely difficult to produce large defect-free single crystals under the appropriate experimental conditions. The difficulty arises because of the combination of low melting point, low specific latent heat of fusion, high vapour pressure, and large expansivity possessed by the solids (Table 4.3), coupled with

| | Triple point (K) | $\alpha_{\text{T.P.}}$ $\overline{(\text{m K}^{-1})}$ | $p_{\text{T.P.}}$ $\overline{(\text{kN m}^{-2})}$ | $U_L^{(\text{T.P.})}$ $\overline{(\text{J mol}^{-1})}$ |
|---|---|---|---|---|
| $^4$He* | (1·0) | ($\sim 25 \cdot 0$) | ($2 \cdot 5 \times 10^3$) | ($\sim 50$) |
| Ne | 24·5 | 6·0 | 43·2 | 346 |
| Ar | 83·8 | 1·6 | 69·0 | 1176 |
| Kr | 116·0 | 1·1 | 73·2 | 1640 |
| Xe | 161·4 | 0·9 | 81·6 | 2300 |

Table 4.3. Properties of the solidified inert gases at their triple points (*some properties of solid helium at 1 K and $2 \cdot 5$ MN m$^{-2}$ are included for comparison—$^4$He does not have a triple point).

a small yield strength at high temperatures and severe brittleness at low temperatures. For example, neon at its triple point has an equilibrium vapour pressure of $\sim 40 \text{ kN m}^{-2}$, a specific latent heat of fusion only 1% that of sodium chloride and a thermal expansivity that is 400 times greater than that of copper at room temperature. Much has been learned recently about crystal growth in general from studies of metals and semi-conductors, and techniques from these studies have been successfully applied to the solidified inert gases. It still remains very difficult, however, to produce a single crystal of dimensions and shape suitable for certain experiments (for example, optical work).

Solid argon has been studied by G. L. Pollack and collaborators. Crystals were grown under varying conditions of rate of growth, temperature gradient at the interface, substrate temperature, chamber geometry and super-saturation, and the grain size was determined as a function of these factors. It was found, for example, that grain size was inversely proportional to the growth rate. Since the likelihood and rate of crystal nucleation depends on the square of the interatomic potential well depth (see § 2.3), the nucleation probability for an argon crystal is about twenty-five times greater than the nucleation probability for a copper crystal under comparable conditions.

Solid argon may be produced by progressive freezing from the melt by a method similar to that of Bridgeman. The liquid argon may be contained in a glass or plastic chamber which is lowered into a liquid nitrogen or other cold bath at a rate which determines the crystal growth. Because the probability of nucleation is high, specimens grown by this method without special precautions originate from many nuclei, resulting in aggregates consisting of many small separate crystals compacted together, instead of the desired single large crystal. However, the research mentioned above has shown that, if a large temperature gradient is maintained at the interface between the crystal and the melt, in the melt itself, and along the walls of the container, nucleation may be localized, and crystal growth controlled.

People usually grow single crystals of metals on a small seed crystal which is oriented at the required angle in the specimen holder. It is very difficult to do this kind of thing with solid argon because of the low temperature. Three alternative methods have been used with some success. O. G. Peterson and co-workers formed a small amount of solid on a copper post in a specimen chamber. This was then annealed at a temperature close to the triple point for some hours. The annealing process increased the probability that the solid displayed only one grain at the solid–liquid interface. This specimen was then used as the seed with which to form the rest of the crystal, grown at a rate of about $0.3 \text{ nm s}^{-1}$. With growth rates as slow as this, a significant amount of annealing of each crystal occurred while it was growing. Before its final cooling, the crystal was first detached from the walls of the specimen tube by filling the chamber with helium exchange gas and then pumping slightly to reduce the vapour pressure. The crystal was then free-standing and could be slowly cooled to the required temperature without too great an internal strain.

In a second method, the author used a tube with a capillary tip in which to grow the specimen (fig. 4.4(a)). Liquid argon was condensed into the tube which was then slowly cooled from the tip upwards. When the argon froze, a number of small crystallites were formed at the tip. These grew up the capillary tube at rates that depended on their orientation with respect to the tube axis. The direction of most rapid growth for solid argon is in the [100] direction perpendicular to the (100) plane), as shown in fig. 4.4(c). Thus if a crystallite exists

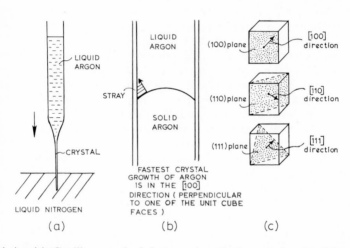

(a)                    (b)                    (c)

Fig. 4.4. (a) Capillary method for growing single crystals of solid argon. (b) A convex interface towards the liquid discourages stray nucleation. (c) Crystallographic planes in a cubic lattice with descriptive Miller indices.

that has a (100) plane perpendicular to the axis of the tube it tends to grow more quickly than its competitors and fills the tube. The length of the capillary should be such that by the time that the solid reaches the end, one crystal will have outgrown all the others. Ideally, the material of the tube should have a smaller thermal conductivity than solid argon or should be heated so that the solid–liquid interface is convex towards the liquid. With this profile any stray crystallites formed would have a much smaller chance of survival (4.4(b)).

A third method, used with some success by W. B. Daniels et al., is to grow the crystal from the melt under high pressure. A krypton specimen was prepared by freezing at $\sim 0 \cdot 23 \text{ GN m}^{-2}$ and then annealed under pressure for three weeks at 166 K, i.e. about 10 K below the melting temperature. It was then cooled to 79 K, the temperature at which experimental observations were made. Care was taken, however, to keep the crystal under positive pressure at all times.

Simmons and others have examined the quality of their solid specimens by X-ray diffraction. Much useful information may also be obtained by thermal etching, i.e., warming the surface of a crystal so that some of the molecules evaporate. Since surface molecules that are on highly defected sites are more loosely bound than those on true crystal faces, they are preferentially evaporated from a free solid surface. Also, because the surface free energy associated with a defect site is larger than that of a true crystal face, the molecules tend to migrate along a polycrystalline surface from the grain boundaries on to the crystal faces. The preferential evaporation and surface migration processes are more rapid in the inert gas solids than in metals because of the relatively weaker intermolecular forces.

Photographs of thermally etched specimens of solid argon taken by Farabaugh and Pollack (1963) are shown in fig. 4.5. The sample that was grown quickly (fig. 4.5(a)) shows a smaller average grain size than the sample grown slowly from the liquid. Because of the high degree of symmetry in the face-centred cubic lattice, the grain boundaries tend to intersect at junctions at which three boundaries meet at an angle of $120°$ to each other. Lighter striations visible on the single crystal faces are probably slip lines, separating regions in the crystal that have the same orientation but are slightly displaced.

A most striking effect (fig. 4.6) is observed when liquid argon is cooled in a vessel in such a way that a solid crust forms on the liquid. As further cooling takes place the liquid contracts, and because the volume is fixed by the crust, the pressure within the liquid becomes less than the equilibrium vapour pressure, causing a vapour bubble to appear below the crust. As the liquid evaporates to fill the vapour bubble, a thin solid shell freezes around it. The bubble is observed to travel down into the melt as a tubule or ' snake ', with a transparent thin-walled solid sheath and an apparently closed tip. The velocity of propagation ($\sim 10^{-2}$ m s$^{-1}$) is determined by the rate of cooling; and the dimensions of the tubule depend on the vapour pressure of the liquid at the melting point, the initial temperature of the melt and the ratio of the latent heat of vaporization to the heat of fusion.

## 4.3. *Nucleation studies*

The nucleation process that initiates crystallization has been studied by D. J. Ball and J. A. Venables, who constructed a liquid-helium stage in an electron-microscope to observe inert gases condensing upon a cold graphite substrate. According to current theory, the rate of nucleation should depend on the adsorption energy, the surface diffusion energy, and the energies associated with various size clusters of gas

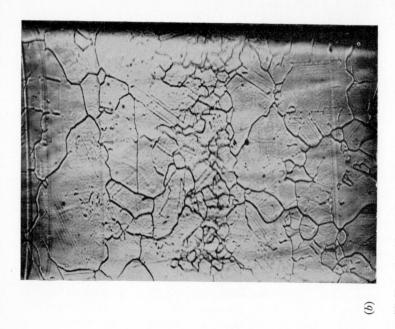

(a)

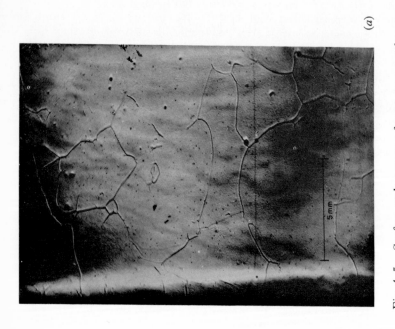

(b)

Fig. 4.5. Surface etch patterns for argon crystals grown at 77 K under identical conditions but at different growth rates (a) 3 $\mu$m s$^{-1}$; (b) 11 $\mu$m s$^{-1}$.

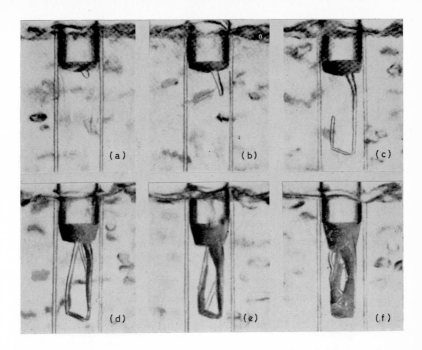

Fig. 4.6. Sequence of vapour snake formation. (a)–(f) Photographs taken at ~1 s intervals.

atoms. Since these energies are known or may easily be calculated for inert gas atoms adsorbed on graphite, the theory may be tested by determining the number density $N_s$, the number of crystallites nucleated per unit area, before the crystals coalesce. To carry out such a test Ball and Venables measured the variation of $N_s$ with the temperature of the substrate, $T$, and the rate of arrival of the inert gas atoms, $R$. According to nucleation theory,

$$(N_s/N_0) = C_i{}^*(R/N_0\nu)i^*/(i^*+1) \exp\left[(E_i{}^*+i^*E_d)/(i^*+1)kT\right] \quad (4.3)$$

where $E_i{}^*$ is the binding energy of an $i^*$ cluster, $E_d$ is the surface diffusion energy, $\nu$ is the adsorbed-atom vibration frequency, $N_0$ is the density of sites at which atoms may be adsorbed and $C_i{}^*$ is a geometrical constant. The value of $i^*$ for which $N_s$ is a minimum is the actual cluster size. For example, if $i^*=2$, this implies that if two atoms are bound together, the addition of a third would form a stable cluster. Thus $i^*$ has a value that is one less than the minimum number of atoms in a stable cluster.

Electron micrographs of the substrate are taken about 15 s after the inert gas is admitted to the cold stage. Nucleation commences within milliseconds of the molecules reaching the surface and initially takes

55

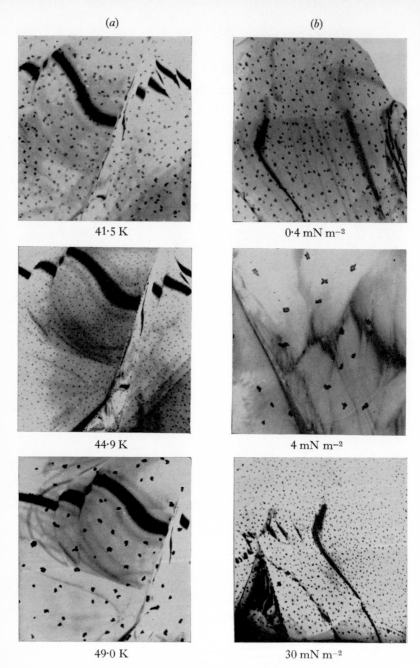

(a)                                                    (b)

41·5 K                                                 0·4 mN m⁻²

44·9 K                                                 4 mN m⁻²

49·0 K                                                 30 mN m⁻²

Fig. 4.7. Electron micrographs of xenon on graphite. (a) Nucleation densities at constant arrival rate but different temperatures ($p \approx 3$ mN m⁻²). (b) Nucleation of molecules at constant temperature but at different arrival rates ($T = 45 \cdot 8$ K).

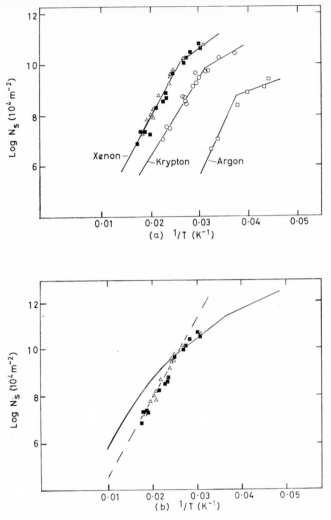

Fig. 4.8. (a) Variation of the saturation density $N_s$ with $1/T$ for argon, krypton and xenon on graphite at $p \approx 4 \, \text{mN m}^{-2}$. (b) Comparison between experimental observations and theoretical predictions for the variation of $N_s$ with $1/T$ for xenon. Continuous line—equation (4.3). Dashed line—equation (4.4). $\triangle$, $\blacksquare$ experimental observations.

place in one plane only as inert gas molecules diffuse on the graphite surface. By the time that the micrographs are taken, the crystallites contain about $10^6$ molecules and are many layers thick. However, $N_s$ will not have changed appreciably since molecules reaching the substrate will join an existing crystallite in preference to initiating further nucleation.

Typical electron micrographs are shown in fig. 4.7. The saturation density $N_s$ is seen to increase as the gas pressure increases and as the temperature of the substrate is lowered. The bands, striations and other features visible in the micrographs are irrelevant and due to electron diffraction from the graphite. The results to date are summarized in fig. 4.8(a).

A marked feature of the behaviour of argon, krypton and xenon is that each exhibits a break in the gradient of log $N_s$ versus $1/T$ within the temperature range studied (20–70 K). Below this transition, $i^* = 2$; thus three atoms are sufficient to form a stable nucleus. Above the transition temperature it appears that growth, not nucleation, is the factor that determines $N_s$. This is because once two nearest neighbour bonds become unstable, all clusters are to some extent unstable, since some steps in the growth process for all clusters add only two nearest neighbour bonds. Above the transition temperature $N_s$ is given by

$$N_s/N_0 \simeq \tfrac{1}{2}(R/N_0\nu) \exp\left[(2E_i^* + E_d)/kT\right] \qquad (4.4)$$

A check of equation (4.4) may be made by evaluating $E_d$ and $E_i^*$ using a Mie–Lennard-Jones potential and comparing the predictions with the experimental observations (fig. 4.8(b)). Agreement is very good and one concludes that nucleation and initial growth processes are better understood in the inert gas crystals than in any other system at present.

## 5.1. *Density and expansivity*

We shall now consider some recent investigations of the lattice properties. Until about 1963, most experiments had been performed on polycrystalline samples and even today it is extremely difficult to produce large single crystals suitable for some types of investigation, for example, optical studies.

Following the adoption of a successful technique for growing single crystals (see §4.2), R. O. Simmons and co-workers have determined the spacing between atoms in a crystal (the X-ray lattice constant) the thermal expansivity and the isothermal compressibility of solid argon. The results are impressive because of the high accuracy (fig. 5.1).

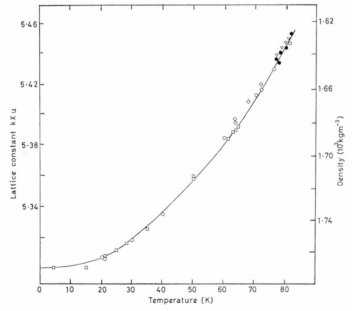

Fig. 5.1. The density and lattice parameter of solid argon. Continuous line—Peterson *et al.* (1966). ● Smith and Chapman (1967). □, ○, earlier X-ray work. ▽, ◇, earlier bulk density determinations. ($1kXu=10\cdot02059$ nm).

For example, the measured lattice constant extrapolated to 0 K is 0·531108 ± 0·000008 nm which is several orders of magnitude more accurate than previous measurements. Five separate measurements on one crystal at 4·2 K taken over a period of nine days during which the crystal was thermally cycled through 80 K had an absolute deviation from the mean value of only 0·000003 nm.

How do the experimental results for density and expansivity compare with theoretical predictions? The reason why a solid expands when heated is that the variation of the interatomic potential with separation is not symmetrical about the minimum value. Consider the potential energy between two argon molecules (fig. 5.2). Neglecting zero point

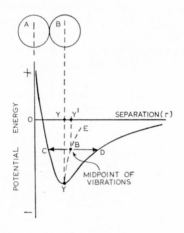

Fig. 5.2. Potential energy as a function of separation for two argon molecules. Expansion occurs on heating because of asymmetry of the potential well.

energy, the equilibrium separation at absolute zero is $OY$. As the temperature is raised both molecules acquire thermal energy and vibrate about their mean positions; thus $B$ oscillates between $C$ and $D$. Because of the asymmetry of the potential curve the midpoint of the vibration is $Y'$ and the separation $O'Y'$ is greater than $OY$. Although other complications arise when considering the assembly of all the molecules in a solid, this is the main reason why a solid expands when heated.

An exact evaluation of the thermal properties of a solid is complicated and only an outline of the argument is given below. A more complete treatment is included in *Gases, Liquids and Solids* by D. Tabor (Penguin), and for a detailed discussion the reader is referred to a more specialized book on the solid state, for example *Introduction to Solid State Physics* by C. Kittel (Wiley).

To calculate the expansion of a lattice one represents the $N$ atoms in a crystal by a system of $3N$ oscillators, by resolving the vibration of each atom into three mutually perpendicular components. Assuming that the motion is simple harmonic, then according to quantum theory only certain energies are allowed. These are caleld eigen-values. The eigen-value of the $i$th oscillator is given by $\epsilon_i = (n + \frac{1}{2}) h\nu_i$ where $\nu_i$ is the frequency of vibration and the integer $n_i$ is the appropriate quantum number ($\frac{1}{2}h\nu_i$ is the zero-point energy).

The total energy of the crystal is the sum of the potential energy and kinetic energy of the lattice, i.e.

$$\epsilon_t = U_0 + \sum_{i=1}^{3N} (n_i + \frac{1}{2}) h\nu_i \qquad (5.1)$$

where $U_0$ is the potential energy of the static lattice. The Helmholtz free energy $F$ (see Appendix) may be obtained from the total eigen-value $\epsilon_t$ since, according to statistical mechanics,

$$F = -kT \ln Z \qquad (5.2)$$

where

$$Z = \sum_{i=1}^{3N} \exp(-\epsilon_t/kT) \qquad (5.3)$$

The total energy may be evaluated by using Boltzmann's law, which states that the number of ocillators in the system with energy $\epsilon_i$ is proportional to $\exp[-\epsilon_i/kT]$. Thus substituting for $\epsilon_t$ from equation (5.1) into equation (5.2) and taking the sum of the geometric progression over the quantum numbers,

$$F = U_0 + \frac{kT}{2} \sum_{i=1}^{3N} \frac{h\nu_i}{kT} + kT \sum_{i=1}^{3N} \ln[1 - \exp(-h\nu_i/kT)] \qquad (5.4)$$

The expression for the general equation of state of a crystal may be obtained from equation (5.4), because

$$p = -\left(\frac{\partial F}{\partial V}\right)_T$$

Differentiating equation (5.4) with respect to volume,

$$p = -\frac{dU_0}{dV} - \sum_{i=1}^{3N} \left[\frac{1}{2} + \frac{1}{[\exp(-h\nu_i/kT) - 1]}\right] \frac{d(h\nu_i)}{dV} \qquad (5.5)$$

If it may be assumed that $U_0$ and $\nu_i$ are functions of volume only, then by defining a new dimensionless parameter $\gamma$ such that

$$\gamma_i = -\frac{d \ln \nu_i}{d \ln V} = -\frac{V}{\nu_i} \cdot \frac{d\nu_i}{dV}$$

61

equation (5.5) thus becomes

$$p + \frac{dU_0}{dV} = \frac{1}{V} \sum_{i=1}^{3N} \gamma_i \{\tfrac{1}{2}h\nu_i + h\nu_i/[\exp(-h\nu_i/kT)-1]\} \quad (5.6)$$

It can be shown that the average energy of a simple harmonic oscillator of frequency $\nu_i$ is $h\nu_i/[\exp(h\nu_i/kT)-1]$. For details see, for example, the references quoted above. $\tfrac{1}{2}h\nu_i$ is just a zero-point energy term (see §2.4.) The summation on the right-hand side of equation (5.6) is therefore the total vibrational energy $E_{\text{vib}}$ of the crystal, assuming that the $N$ atoms behave as $3N$ independent oscillators, and

$$pV + V\frac{dU_0}{dV} = \sum_{i=1}^{3N} \gamma_i \epsilon_{\text{vib}}$$

This is the general equation of state of a crystal. The expansivity is defined by

$$\alpha = \frac{1}{V}\left(\frac{\partial V}{\partial T}\right)_p$$

Thus it depends on both the energy of the static lattice and the vibrational energy $E_{\text{vib}}$.

The calculation of the static lattice potential has been discussed in §4.1. The symmetry of the crystal structure of the solidified inert gases and the relative simplicity and short-range of the intermolecular forces makes the computation relatively simple. Summations of intermolecular potentials over a face-centred cubic lattice have been tabulated for various forms of the Mie–Lennard-Jones potential.

Before the value for $E_{\text{vib}}$ in equation (5.6) can be calculated, the frequency spectrum must be known, i.e. the frequencies of all the oscillators or else the distribution of oscillator frequencies amongst the range of possible values. The real frequency spectrum of even a simple solid is very complicated (fig. 5.3($a$)) and $E_{\text{vib}}$ is difficult to evaluate. For this reason, most theoretical treatments make use of simple approximate representations of the frequency distribution.

The simplest form is the Einstein model, in which all the vibration frequencies are assumed to be equal to one constant $\nu_E$ (fig. 5.3($b$)). A parameter $\Theta_E$, the Einstein characteristic temperature, is introduced, defined by

$$\Theta_E = h\nu_E/k$$

Hence

$$\gamma = -\,\mathrm{d}\ln\nu_i/\mathrm{d}\ln V = -\,\mathrm{d}\ln\nu_E/\mathrm{d}\ln V = \gamma_E$$

and the general equation of state, equation (5.6), becomes

$$pV + V\frac{dU_0}{dV} = \gamma_E f(T/\Theta) \quad (5.7)$$

where $f(T/\Theta)$ denotes a function of the temperature and $\Theta_E$.

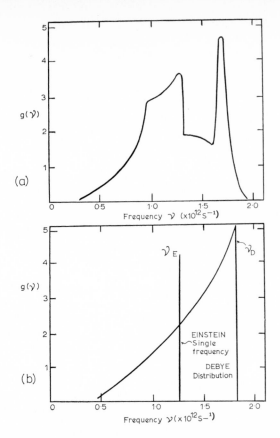

Fig. 5.3. Vibration frequency spectra for face-centred cubic lattice. (*a*) Full frequency distribution (calculated). (*b*) Einstein and Debye approximations.

The Einstein model assumes that all the atoms vibrate at the same frequency and move independently of each other. This is unrealistic because in practice a range of frequencies is possible and interactions take place between the individual oscillators.

A slightly different approach is due to Debye. He suggested that a solid be treated as an 'elastic continuum' in which standing waves (lattice waves) could exist. Each wave of frequency $v$ behaves exactly as a quantum oscillator of the same frequency and the net vibration of each atom may be represented by a combination of a large number of waves. A distribution function $f_D(v)$ is introduced so that

$$f_D(v)\Delta v = \lim_{N \to \infty} [N(v)\Delta v/N]$$

represents the number of waves with frequencies which lie in the range

63

$\nu$ to $\nu + \Delta\nu$, and the function $f_D(\nu)$ is normalized so that

$$\int_0^\infty f_D(\nu)\Delta\nu = 3\,N$$

because there are $3\,N$ degrees of freedom (oscillators) in the lattice. The main feature of this model is that it allows a range of frequencies within the lattice (fig. 5.3($b$)), compared with the single frequency used in the Einstein approximation. Again, a characteristic temperature $\Theta_D$ may be introduced, defined by

$$\Theta_D = h\nu_D/k$$

and

$$-\,\mathrm{d}\ln\nu_D/\mathrm{d}\ln V = \gamma_D$$

Hence the equation of state (5.6) becomes

$$\mathrm{d}V + V\frac{\mathrm{d}U_0}{\mathrm{d}V} = \gamma_D f(T/\Theta_D) \tag{5.8}$$

Before discussing how well these equations describe the expansivity and other properties of the solid there is one more useful relationship that may be derived from equation (5.6). If it can be assumed that all the vibrational frequencies are equal, then

$$pV = V\frac{\mathrm{d}U_0}{\mathrm{d}V} = \gamma E_{\mathrm{vib}}$$

Differentiating with respect to $T$ at constant volume

$$V\left(\frac{\partial p}{\partial T}\right)_V = \gamma\left(\frac{\partial E_{\mathrm{vib}}}{\partial T}\right)_V = \gamma C_v \tag{5.9}$$

because the heat supplied at constant volume is equal to the change in $E_{\mathrm{vib}}$. Since it can be shown that

$$\left(\frac{\partial p}{\partial T}\right)_V = -\left(\frac{\partial p}{\partial V}\right)_T\left(\frac{\partial V}{\partial T}\right)_p = \frac{\alpha}{k_T} \tag{5.10}$$

where $\alpha$ is the expansivity and $k_T$ is the isothermal compressibility, from equations (5.9) and (5.10)

$$\gamma = \alpha V/k_T C_v = \alpha V/k_s C_p \tag{5.11}$$

where $k_s$ is the adiabatic compressibility and $C_p$ is the molar heat capacity at constant pressure. Equation (5.11) is known as Grüneisen's law and $\gamma$ is the 'Grüneisen' parameter. From experimental determinations of $\alpha$ and the other parameters, the constancy of $\gamma$ and hence the validity of the Einstein model may be tested.

Theoretical estimates of the expansivity of solid argon are compared with the results of experimental measurements in fig. 5.4. As might

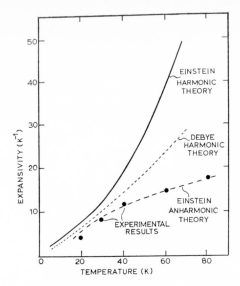

Fig. 5.4. Comparison of theoretical predictions of the expansivity ($\times 10^4$) of solid argon with experimental values.

be expected, computations based on the Debye model are in better agreement than those based on the Einstein model. However, both appear to be seriously in error at higher temperatures. As we shall explain, this is probably due to the neglect of anharmonic effects when calculating the lattice vibrations. Consider the molecule $B$ vibrating at a temperature $T$ in fig. 5.3. Suppose that the thermal energy $U_B$ at $T$ may be described in terms of the displacement $x$ from the equilibrium separation by

$$U_B = Ax + Bx^2 + Cx^3 + \ldots$$

The first coefficient $A = 0$, since $(\partial U_B/\partial x) = 0$ when $x = 0$. The second term describes harmonic motion about the equilibrium separation because the restoring force for a displacement $x$, $(\partial U_B/\partial x) = -2Bx$ and is therefore proportional to $x$. If it is assumed that $U_B \simeq Bx^2$ (the harmonic approximation), solution of the wave equation for the crystal and calculation of the lattice properties is relatively straightforward, but inclusion of anharmonic terms, i.e. $Cx^3$ and higher, makes the problem considerably harder. The success of the anharmonic calculation using the Einstein frequency distribution to describe the expansivity of solid argon (see fig. 5.4) makes one wonder whether perhaps the anharmonic effect is more important than the choice of frequency model.

It is interesting to note that some anharmonic effects are introduced in the Grüneisen theory. The frequency of vibration $\nu$ depends on the second differential of the potential with respect to the volume, and $\gamma$ depends on the third differential. Thus, in effect, terms beyond the second are included in the expansion for the harmonic and from this viewpoint the theory may be regarded as quasi harmonic. The variation of Grüneisen parameter $\gamma$ with temperature is shown in fig. 5.5, where once again the anharmonic theories appear to be in close agreement with experiment.

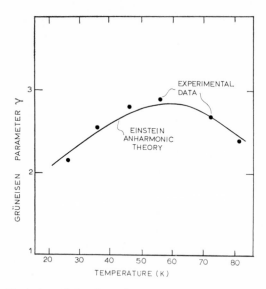

Fig. 5.5. Variation of the Grüneisen parameter $\gamma$ with temperature—
comparison of theory with experiment.

## 5.2. *Molar heat capacity*

Heat supplied at constant volume to a solid is used entirely in increasing the vibrational energy, hence the molar heat capacity is

$$C_v = (\partial U / \partial T)_V$$

The molar heat capacity at constant pressure is slightly larger and it may be shown that $C_p - C_v = TV\alpha^2/k_T$ where $k_T$ is the compressibility and $V$ is the molar volume.

Dulong and Petit suggested, on the basis of the evidence available, that $C_v = 3R = 24 \cdot 9$ J mol$^{-1}$ K$^{-1}$ for a monatomic solid. This value is only reached above a certain temperature characteristic of the individual solid, and below this temperature, the frequency distribution of the crystal oscillators has to be considered.

Following a similar discussion to that contained in the previous section, for the Einstein model, each oscillator has an energy $u_i$ given by

$$u_i = h\nu_i/[\exp(-h\nu_i/kT) - 1]$$

and for the $3\,N$ oscillators

$$U = 3\,N\,u_i$$

At high temperatures, this tends to $3\,N\,kT$ in agreement with the Dulong and Petit law but at low temperatures, $C_v$ falls off as $\exp(-h\nu/kT)$. Experimentally $C_v$ is found to vary as $T^3$, i.e. more slowly than predicted by the above theory. Using the Debye model, $C_v$ for a solid is found to depend only on the characteristic frequency $\nu_D$. Thus if $C_v$ for different solids is plotted against $kT/h\nu_D = T/\Theta_D$ all the points should lie on a single curve.

The molar heat capacities of argon, krypton, xenon and neon have been measured. The results may be conveniently described in terms of the Debye temperature $\Theta_D$ extrapolated to absolute zero $(\Theta_D)_{T=0\,\mathrm{K}}$. To establish $(\Theta_D)_{T=0\,\mathrm{K}}$ accurately it is necessary to determine $C_v$ at very low temperatures (at least below $\Theta_D/50$, which means measurements at temperatures below $\sim 2$ K). L. Finegold has recently completed a series of measurements that allows accurate estimates of $(\Theta_D)_{T=0\,\mathrm{K}}$ for argon and krypton to be made. The results, plotted in reduced forms, are compared in fig. 5.6 with theoretical calculations based on the Mie–Lennard-Jones (6,12) potential in the harmonic approximation by G. K. Horton and J. W. Leech. Horton and Leech systematically examined the effect of varying the potential and also the number of nearest neighbour shells included in the calculations. For

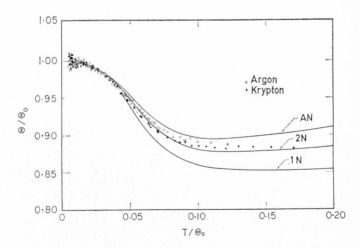

Fig. 5.6. Comparison of reduced heat capacities of argon and krypton with theoretical predictions (Finegold and Phillips 1969).

67

low values of $T/\Theta_D$ they found that it made very little difference whether they considered nearest neighbours only (1 $N$), included next nearest neighbours (2 $N$), or all neighbours ($AN$). Since there appears to be little difference between the theoretical or experimental results for argon and krypton, this is an indication that the effects of zero-point energy are small. The experimental values appear in fact to fall between the 1 $N$ and $AN$ calculations, being slightly higher but in basic agreement with the 2 $N$ computation.

The effect of including temperature-dependent anharmonic effects in the calculations by Horton and Leech would be to raise the harmonic reduced $\Theta_D - T$ curves shown in fig. 5.6, but the change would be quite small. Since the $AN$ calculation does not give the best agreement with experiment, one must assume that the potential must be corrected, either by altering its shape or by including three-body interactions. A detailed examination of $\Theta - T$ plots for all the solids suggests that different potentials are needed to cover different temperature regions. E. A. Guggenheim and M. L. McGlashan have pointed out that the Mie–Lennard-Jones potential exaggerates the effect of distant neighbours. A slight modification of the potential at intermediate distances (fig. 5.7), such as suggested by B. J. Alder and R. H. Paulson, would

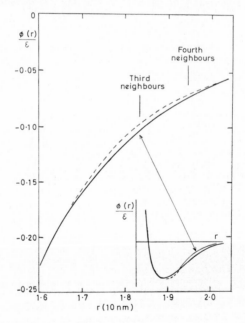

Fig. 5.7. A partially modified Mie–Lennard-Jones (12, 6) potential that would stabilize face-centred cubic argon (Alder and Paulson 1965). The inset shows in an exaggerated manner how the modification would change the potential.

reduce the influence of third and fourth neighbours and would also make face-centred cubic argon more stable than the hexagonal close-packed form (see § 4.1). Such a modification is acceptable because although it would change the form of the atomic interactions it would have no appreciable effect on those virial coefficients that are sensitive to the potential in this distance range, and also would lie within the limits of experimental error.

## 5.3. *Thermal conductivity*

Heat is conducted in metals both by electrons, and by thermal waves called phonons. The process is really rather complicated. But in a solidified inert gas there are no free electrons and thermal energy is transferred through the lattice solely by means of the phonons which are associated with the lattice vibrations.

In the harmonic approximation, the molecules are assumed to perform simple harmonic oscillations about their lattice sites. In this case the potential energy of a molecule displaced from its equilibrium lattice position is proportional to the square of the displacement. Mathematical analysis shows that energy transfer between the lattice modes is not possible, as a consequence of neglecting higher order terms (i.e. terms other than the harmonic ones) in the energy. Physically this means that there is no interaction between phonons and therefore that heat transfer takes place at approximately the speed of sound, which is the unmodified speed of the phonons.

To account for the observed thermal conductivities of the solidified inert gases, anharmonicity in the intermolecular potential equivalent to a coupling between the lattice modes must be properly considered. This is done by including items other than the harmonic term in the expression for the potential energy. At high temperatures i.e., $T \gg \Theta_D$ thermal conductivity is dominated by interactions involving three phonons—called *Umklapp processes*, for which the thermal conductivity $\lambda \propto 1/T$. This law is in good agreement with the results of measurements on the solidified inert gases (fig. 5.8) and in fact extends down to $T \sim \Theta_D/3$. At lower temperatures, the mean free paths associated with the phonons increase and Umklapp processes become less probable. It may be shown that the conductivity depends approximately on $[\exp (\Theta_D/2T)]/T$, assuming that scattering from defects from within the crystal may be neglected. As the temperature is lowered further, scattering from the crystal imperfections becomes increasingly important. The thermal conductivity passes through a maximum ($\sim \Theta_D/20$) and then decreases with decreasing temperature.

The mean free path $l$ of the phonons may be estimated by analogy with a gas, where the transfer is by molecular collisions. For poor conductors such as the solidified inert gases

$$\lambda \approx C \cdot vl/3$$

69

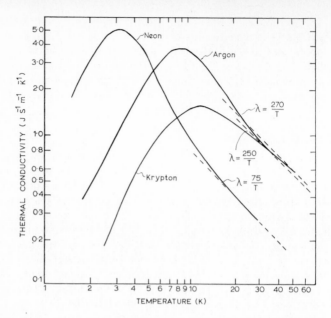

Fig. 5.8.  Thermal conductivity of solid argon, krypton and neon.
(G. K. White and S. B. Woods.)

where $C$ is the heat capacity *per unit volume* and $v$ is the speed of sound. From the available data for the solids $l \approx 10^{-6}$ m at 2 K.   It is extremely difficult to produce strain and defect free specimens at this temperature since annealing processes are so slow.   It therefore seems likely that, since it is known that lattice waves are strongly scattered by grain boundaries and other crystal imperfections, the results of present measurements at low temperatures depend more on the crystallization conditions and thermal history of the sample than on the lattice itself.

## 5.4. *Vacancies and diffusion*

Studies on solids have shown that at reasonably high temperatures, atomic diffusion plays an important role in determining properties, and that diffusion is linked with the presence of vacancies or interstitial atoms in the solid.   Even in the equilibrium state, lattice defects are bound to arise close to the triple point, because of the increase in entropy with which this is accompanied.   The process may be considered to start at the surface (fig. 5.9) as some atoms leave their original positions and move to new situations on the surface.   Atoms from deeper layers can then move into the vacancies created.   The vacancies thus appear to diffuse into the interior of the sample.

Although the introduction of vacancies causes the internal energy $U$ to rise by an amount $\Delta U$, there is also an increase in the disorder of the

70

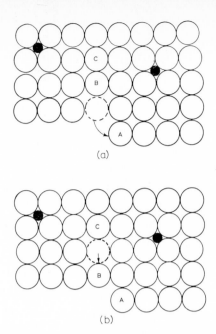

(a)

(b)

Fig. 5.9. Vacancies may be introduced into a solid from a crystal boundary. (a) A vacancy is formed by the displacement of molecule (A). (b) The vacancy then diffuses into the crystal by displacement of other atoms. (The smaller molecules (●) are shown in interstitial positions.)

crystal, and hence the entropy. As long as $T\Delta S > \Delta U$, creation of vacancies reduces the Helmholtz free energy $F = U - TS$, and makes the crystal more stable. If the free energy associated with a vacancy in the crystal is $g_V$, and in equilibrium there are $n$ vacancies in a crystal of $N$ atoms, then

$$n/N = \exp\left(-g_V/kT\right) = \exp\left(-E_V/RT\right) \qquad (5.12)$$

where $E_V$ is the energy required to create a mole of vacancies.

Calculations of the formation energies suggest that vacancies are the only important point defects present in the solidified inert gases since the energy required to form interstitials is considerably higher. H. R. Glyde has estimated that $g_V = (7\cdot95 - 16\cdot7RT)$ J mol$^{-1}$ (for solid argon), assuming that the atoms interact with a Mie–Lennard-Jones potential. There are two experimental methods that have been used to determine the actual vacancy concentration. The first is based on specific heat measurements carried out over most of the solid range, in which the heat capacity at constant volume was found to rise more rapidly near the triple point than would be expected from any reasonable anharmonic theory (fig. 5.10). The extra contribution due to the

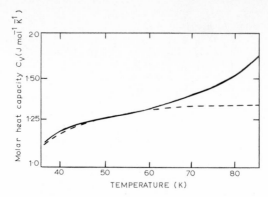

Fig. 5.10. Molar heat capacity of solid argon at constant volume. Continuous line—experimental values (R. H. Beaumont, H. Chihara and J. A. Morrison). Dashed line—theoretical estimate assuming the absence of vacancies.

formation of $n$ vacancies may be estimated from equation (5.12) since

$$\mathrm{d}(\Delta U)/\mathrm{d}T = \mathrm{d}(ng_V)/\mathrm{d}T = \mathrm{d}[Ng_V \exp{(-g_V/kT)}]/\mathrm{d}T$$

$$= R(g_V/kT)^2 \exp{(-g_V/kT)} \qquad (5.13)$$

Therefore by comparing the observed heat capacity with the theoretical estimate, the vacancy concentration may be estimated via equation (5.13). The original estimate made by this method gave a value for $n/N$ of 1·5% at the triple point, which is several orders of magnitude larger than would be expected by analogy with metals. Subsequent estimates have reduced this to $\sim 0\cdot 1$ per cent.

A more direct method for estimating vacancy concentration is to compare the results of X-ray measurements with direct determinations of the bulk density. In the X-ray method, the positions of Laue spots diffracted from a single crystal of the solid are analysed and used to find the intermolecular spacing in the solid. This work has been described in § 5.1. In the bulk density method a specimen of solid argon is slowly grown from the liquid in a glass bulb of known volume (fig. 5.11). After annealing, the specimen is allowed to evaporate into an expansion volume, where the pressure and temperature of the gas is measured. From a knowledge of the density of the gas, the mass of argon and hence the density of the solid is determined.

These measurements may then be compared with X-ray values as follows. If $n$ is the number of vacancies in a crystal containing $N$ atomic sites, then

$$(\rho_x - \rho)/\rho_x = n/N$$

where $\rho$ is the bulk density and $\rho_x$ is the density deduced from the

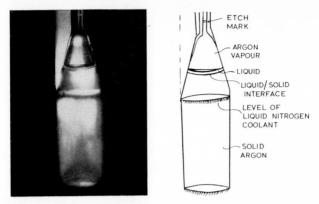

Fig. 5.11.  Formation of a specimen of solid argon in a glass bulb for a bulk density determination.

lattice parameter. For argon (face-centred cubic), $\rho_x = 4M/N_A a^3$, where $M$ is the molecular weight, $a$ the lattice constant and $N_A$ Avogadro's constant. There seems to be little likelihood that the number of vacancies near the triple point of solid argon is as high as has been suggested on the basis of the analysis of heat capacity data described above. Because the errors in X-ray and bulk density measurements overlap, it is not possible to evaluate the equilibrium vacancy concentration specifically, but only to set an upper limit to its possible value. At 81·7 K, for example, $n/N \leq 0·12\%$, which is equivalent to $n/N < 0·13\%$ at the triple point. Since $n/N = \exp\left(-g_V/kT\right)$, this implies that $g_V \geq 18·8$ kJ/mol$^{-1}$ which is consistent with the two-body force calculation by Glyde in which a theoretical value of $g_V = (7·95 - 16·7RT)$ J mol$^{-1}$ was obtained. Recent measurements have attempted to determine the vacancy concentration in rods of solidified inert gas by carrying out length and lattice parameter measurements simultaneously, but these have not yet reached the stage where firm conclusions may be drawn.

At temperatures near the triple point the vacancies in a solid move relatively freely. A vacancy moves a distance equivalent to the inter-molecular spacing if an adjacent molecule jumps into it. The energy required for such a jump $q$, the activation energy, is large compared with the average vibrational energy of the molecules, and the number of atoms in a crystal of $N$ atoms that possess at least this energy is proportional to $\exp\left(-q/kT\right) = \exp\left(-Nq/RT\right)$.

The diffusion coefficient $D_V$ is approximately proportional to this factor: $D_V = D_0 \exp\left(-Nq/RT\right) = D_0 \exp\left(-Q/RT\right)$ where $D_0$ is a constant, nearly independent of temperature.

A similar type of argument may be applied to self-diffusion in a solid, i.e. the process by which atoms move through a lattice of identical

73

atoms, which may be studied experimentally, for example, by using radioactive isotope atoms of the pure substance as tracers. Here, however, the coefficient of diffusion $D_s$ is smaller, since an atom can only jump at a time when there happens to be a vacancy beside it. $D_s$ is proportional both to the vacancy diffusion coefficient $D_V$ and to the relative number of vacancies $n/N = \exp(-g_V/kT)$. It may be written in the form

$$D_s = D'_0 \exp(-Q'/RT) \tag{5.13}$$

where $Q' = E_V + Q$. Studies of self-diffusion in the solidified inert gases are particularly valuable because calculations of the activation energy may be compared with experimental results as a realistic test of the various mechanisms and models proposed for diffusion. By contrast, in metals there is much greater uncertainty in the interatomic potential.

The experimental determination of the self-diffusion coefficient of solid argon is worth studying in some detail because of the technical difficulties involved, typical of those encountered in experiments with the solidified inert gases. Conventional methods used with metals, involving handling and sectioning techniques, cannot be applied to the solidified inert gases because of their very high vapour pressures near the triple points (argon 69 kN m$^{-2}$ at 84 K), and because they solidify at cryogenic temperatures. A further difficulty is that of preparing specimens with well-defined surface areas for diffusion.

The apparatus is shown in fig. 5.12. Thin solid specimens of argon (thickness $\sim 10~\mu$m) are deposited directly from the vapour phase on to a well-defined cold area on the base of chamber $S$. To initiate the diffusion process a tracer mixture containing $^{36}$Ar, prepared in volume $T$, is exchanged with the vapour above the solid via needle valves $N_1$ and $N_3$. Slow gravitational displacement of the mercury column controlled by valve $F$ allows this operation to be carried out over a period of $\sim 10^2$ s under constant pressure conditions. The time taken to exchange the vapour has to be short relative to the duration of the experiment, in order that the start of the diffusion process is well defined. Because the mixing in the vapour phase ($D_{\text{vap}} \approx 10^{-6}$ m$^2$ s$^{-1}$) is fast relative to diffusion rates in the solid ($D_s \approx 10^{-15}$ m$^2$ s$^{-1}$), the system is equivalent to a semi-infinite solid in contact with a well-stirred fluid (fig. 5.13).

Diffusion then takes place into the solid and the isotopic concentration in the vapour phase decreases with time, at a rate dependent on the solid diffusion coefficient. Small samples of the vapour ($\sim 10^{16}$ atoms) are extracted at regular intervals by partially opening needle value $N_2$ and leaking it into volume $J$. Each sample is analysed by means of the mass spectrometer $K$. The diffusion coefficient is determined from the rate at which the vapour concentration decreases.

Ideally, experimental investigations of diffusion should be carried

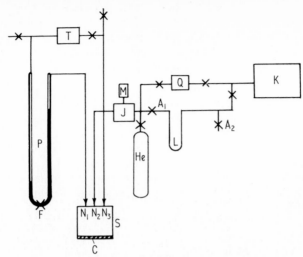

Fig. 5.12. General arrangement of apparatus used for studies of diffusion in solidified inert gases: $A_1$, $A_2$, needle (Hoke) valves; $C$, solid argon specimen; $F$, vapour transfer control valve; He, helium cylinder; $J$, expansion volume; $K$, Nier-type mass spectrometer; $L$, activated charcoal; $M$, Pirani gauge; $N_1$, $N_2$, $N_3$, needle valves; $P$, mercury column used to transfer vapour; $Q$, calibration volume; $S$, diffusion chamber; $T$, tracer mixture.

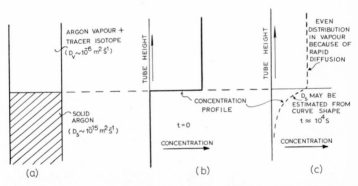

Fig. 5.13. (a) System of vapour in thermal equilibrium with solid is equivalent to well-stirred liquid in contact with semi-infinite solid. (b) Concentration profile of isotope at $t = 0$. (c) Concentration profile some time later during experiment.

out on single crystal specimens with well-defined surface areas. However, preliminary investigations showed that it was not possible to grow single crystal thin films either directly or on a substrate, i.e. epitaxially. Large grain crystals, with diameters about 10 times the thickness, were obtained by annealing to equilibrium. These were used as specimens and the effect of grain boundaries accounted for by means of a correction.

The activation energy for grain boundary and surface diffusion is about 0·5 that for lattice diffusion via vacancies, so that

$$D_{\text{G.B.}} \approx 10^6 D_s \approx 10^3 D_{\text{vap.}}$$

Thus for thin specimens the tracer concentration in the boundaries will rapidly reach equilibrium with the vapour. The effect of the grain boundaries is to increase the effective surface area of the solid exposed to the vapour by an amount $A_B$, the area associated with the grain boundaries. The true surface area for diffusion is then $A = A_s + A_B$, where $A_B$ is the surface area of the copper block.

The effect of grain growth on the effective surface area for diffusion is given in fig. 5.14, where results for runs on specimens which had

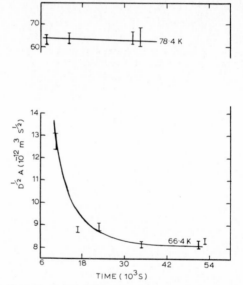

Fig. 5.14. Variation of $D_s^{1/2}A$ with specimen anneal time at 66·4 K and 78·4 K (specimen thickness 11·6 $\mu$m). (E.H.C. Parker *et al.*)

been grown and subsequently annealed at $T = 78·4$ and $66·4$ K are shown. $D_s^{1/2}(A_s + A_B)$ is plotted as a function of the time $t_a$ during which the specimen was annealed prior to the experiment. Since all the measurements were carried out on specimens of the same thickness ($l = 12$ $\mu$m) and surface area $A_s$, the observed decrease in $D_s^{1/2}(A_s + A_B)$ at 66 K must be due to recrystallization processes causing grain-growth and hence reducing $A_B$. From fig. 5.14 it may be seen that when $t_a > 6$ hours, $A_B$ appears to have reached an equilibrium value. Grain-growth at 78 K is so rapid that equilibrium is reached quickly and

$D_s^{1/2}A$ does not appear to change significantly during the range of $t_a$ studied.

Previous investigations have shown that in thin well-annealed samples the grain boundaries traverse the specimen in the shortest possible direction, and thus the grain-boundary area $A_B$ is proportional to the specimen thickness. If $d$ is the average grain diameter of the crystal, $A_B = A_s(4l/d)$ and the total effective surface is $A = A_s + A_B = A_s(1 + 4l/d)$. In fig. 5.15, $D_s^{1/2}A$ is plotted versus $l$ for measurements made at three temperatures. That the points for each temperature lie on a straight line within experimental error confirms that $A_B$ depends only on the sample thickness over the small range of $l$ studied. Using the value of $A_B$ determined from fig. 5.14, $D_s^{1/2}A$ and hence $D_s$ are determined $(D_s \approx 0.0002 \exp(3600/RT) \approx 10^{-15} \text{ m}^2 \text{ s}^{-1}$ for self diffusion in solid argon.)

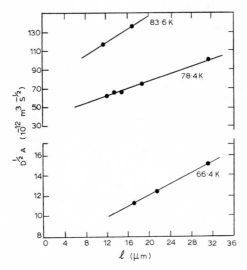

Fig. 5.15. Dependence of $D_s^{1/2}A$ on thickness $l$ for well-annealed specimens.

## 5.5. *Other solid-state properties*

Several other important theoretical and experimental investigations of the solidified inert gases are at present in progress. Studies of inert gas crystals such as solid argon are ideal for investigations into the effects of defects upon lattice vibrations because so much is already known about the behaviour of the perfect lattice. Another advantage that inert gas crystals offer is that, because the polarizabilities of the molecules are small, simple approximate methods may be used to treat the influence of polarization effects on the lattice vibrations (see § 8.6). Luminescence studies on condensed argon, krypton and xenon suggest that laser action might be produced by excitation with an electron beam.

Also of great importance have been some recent determinations of phonon properties by coherent inelastic neutron scattering—a technique similar to X-ray diffraction. In two experiments, crystals of krypton and of neon were grown under pressure (see § 4.2), in a cryostat mounted on a triple-axis crystal spectrometer at the Brookhaven High Flux Beam Reactor. The energies of the phonons created in the specimen by coherent inelastic scattering of the neutrons were determined using a 'constant $Q$' technique with fixed incident neutron energies in the range 20–45 meV. In this method the *momentum* $Q$ transferred between the incident neutrons and the solid is kept constant, while the *energy* of the neutrons is varied over a range of values within which the energy transfer equals the phonon energy. By this technique it is possible to study phonons of chosen wavelengths.

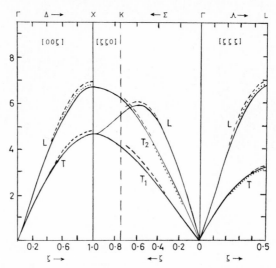

Fig. 5.16. Theoretical and experimental phonon dispersion curves for neon. Continuous line—experimental (J. A. Leake *et al.* 1969). Dashed line—theoretical (self-consistent phonon approximation). Dotted line—theoretical (harmonic approximation).

The results for neon are compared in fig. 5.16 with calculations based on the harmonic approximation or the 'self-consistent phonon approximation'. The latter takes into account effects due to zero-point energy and thermal motion of the atoms and may be compared directly with the experimental data without arbitrary scaling. The former have to be scaled to correspond to the experimental conditions.

Figure 5.16 is complicated and it would not be appropriate to describe the significance of the different curves and 'branches' here.

The important result is that accord between theory and experiment is very good; in particular, the curve shapes seem to be in good agreement. It is possible to make a detailed comparison of the 'experimental' intermolecular force constants taken from fig. 5.16 with those that have been calculated directly from a pair potential energy function. The results are in reasonable agreement with either first and second neighbour, or all neighbour calculations, although slightly better in the latter case (see § 5.2). It would appear, however, that one of the components of the interatomic force constant has a larger negative value than can be accounted for using a (12,6) Mie–Lennard-Jones potential. Since this constant is associated with interactions that are explicitly non-central, this may be taken as an indication that deformation of the outer electron wave-functions of the neon molecules in a compressed crystal causes a significant appearance of non-central forces. Further neutron scattering experiments of this type, particularly on the heavier solids, should yield a great deal of useful information.

There is a great deal of experimental and theoretical work yet to be done before questions concerning the magnitude and hence importance of three-body forces in the crystal lattice are resolved. Determination of elastic properties, including for example, the Cauchy relations $C_{11}$, $C_{12}$ and $C_{44}$ (elastic constants for different directions within the lattice), and vacancy formation energy, should help clarify this issue. It is still not fully established to what extent a simple two-body potential is capable of describing lattice properties accurately, or even how the parameters in these potentials are best chosen. Molecular beam experiments and direct calculations of the polarizabilities should help provide some of these answers.

In spite of these uncertainties, the inert gas crystals remain a most rewarding area of study in solid state physics, because they correspond much more than any other solid systems to 'ideal solids'.

# CHAPTER 6
## liquids

### 6.1. *Introduction*

IN previous chapters, the properties of gases and of solids have been examined. These may be regarded as being reasonably well understood in terms of molecular theory. Liquids on the other hand, have proved to be extremely difficult. In this chapter, we outline the basic problems and examine some of the ingenious attempts that have been made to solve them.

The discussion here will be limited to the equilibrium properties. Much effort has been devoted to trying to understand transport phenomena such as viscosity and diffusion, but the theories tend to be extremely complicated. For our present purposes it will be quite enough to attempt to relate the observed equilibrium behaviour of a liquid to the interactions that occur at the molecular level. The aim therefore is to find expressions which describe bulk properties in terms of molecular parameters.

As has already been pointed out in § 2.5, the equation of state relating $p$, $V$ and $T$ does not fully describe a thermodynamic system since it does not give information concerning the energy-derived properties, for example the specific heat capacity, or the state of equilibrium. It is more valuable to calculate the Helmholtz free energy $F$ of a fluid (see Appendix) because from this all properties, including the equation of state, may be deduced. This is the fundamental task of statistical mechanics—to determine how $F$ depends on $V$ and $T$, given the distribution of molecules in a system and the forces acting between them. The free energy is defined by

$$F = U - TS \qquad (6.1)$$

where $U$ is the internal energy and $S$ is the entropy, and therefore for a small reversible isothermal change in which work is done by increasing the volume by an amount $dV$,

$$dF = dU = -p \, dV$$

If the dependence of $F$ on volume and temperature is known, then the equation of state, relating $p$, $V$ and $T$ is also known:

$$(\partial F/\partial V)_T = -p \qquad (6.2)$$

From equations (6.1) and (6.2) all the other properties of a liquid may be deduced. For example, the volume expansitivity $\alpha_T = (1/V)(\partial V/\partial T)_p$ the entropy $S = -(\partial F/\partial T)_V$, and

$$C_V = (\partial Q/\partial T)_V = (\partial U/\partial T)_V.$$

There are two useful expressions that provide bridges between the macroscopic and microscopic. The first is Clausius' Virial Theorem for an assembly of $N$ molecules:

$$pV = NkT + \tfrac{1}{3} \overline{\sum_{\text{pairs}} r_{ij} \cdot Z(r_{ij})} \tag{6.3}$$

The second term on the right-hand side takes account of the inter-actions between molecules and hence is a correction term to the ideal gas equation $pV = NkT$. $Z(r_{ij})$ represents the force between the $i$th and $j$th molecules, distance $r_{ij}$ apart. The summation is carried out for all pairs of the molecules and the solidus indicates that the value to be used is averaged over time and position. The Virial Equation as given in the form of equation (6.3) is applicable to a system of molecules which interact with central additive forces, i.e. the origins of the force act as if located at the centres of molecules and the net force acting on a given molecule is the sum of the contributions from all of the other molecules.

Each molecular configuration lasts only about $10^{-13}$ s, before the positions change due to thermal motion. During the period of an actual measurement therefore the molecular distribution changes many times. The measured value is a mean value, averaged over time. Since some configurations are more probable than others, when calculating an averaged property, the contribution made by each configuration has to be weighted by the appropriate factor.

The calculation of the mean value is relatively simple in principle. A co-ordinate system can be set up and used to calculate the positions and momenta of all the molecules at a given instant of time. The likelihood of each distribution may then be found using the normal laws of probability. A single representative molecule in the liquid $(i)$ requires three position and three momentum co-ordinates to fully specify its motion. A probability density can then be defined $f(x_i)$, such that $[f(x_i) \cdot dx_i]$ represents the probability that the molecule labelled $i$ is between $x_i$ and $x_i + dx_i$. Similarly, the probability that the $i$th molecule is defined by position co-ordinates $x_i$, $y_i$, $z_i$ and momentum co-ordinates $p_{xi}$, $p_{yi}$, $p_{zi}$ is

$$f(x_i, y_i, z_i, p_{x_i}, p_{y_i}, p_{z_i}) \, dx_i \, dy_i \, dz_i \, dp_{x_i} \, dp_{y_i} \, dp_{z_i}$$

Extrapolating to all $N$ molecules in the system, the probability that

81

molecule 1 is defined by $x_1, y_1, z_1, p_{x_1}, p_{y_1}, p_{z_2}$

molecule 2 is defined by $x_2, y_2, z_2, p_{x_2}, p_{y_2}, p_{z_2}$

.
.
.
.

and

molecule $N$ is defined by $x_N, y_N, z_N, p_{x_N}, p_{y_N}, p_{z_N}$

is given by

$$f(x_1, x_2 \ldots x_N, y_1, y_2, \ldots y_N, z_1, z_2, \ldots z_N, p_{x_1}, p_{x_2} \ldots p_{xN},$$
$$p_{y_1}, \ldots p_{yN}, p_{z_1}, \ldots p_{zN}) \, (dx, \ldots dx_N, dy, \ldots dy_N, dz_1, \ldots dz_N,$$
$$dp_{x_1} \ldots dp_{xN}, dp_{y_1} \ldots dp_{yN}, dp_{z_1} \ldots dp_{zN}) \tag{6.4}$$

Because this is such a large and unwieldy expression, it is convenient to introduce a shortened notation

$$f_N \, dV_N \, dP_N$$

where $f_N$ represents $f(x_i, x_2 \ldots p_{zN})$, $dV_N$ represents $(dx_1 \ldots dx_N)$ and $dP_N$ represents $(dp_{x_1} \ldots dp_{xN})$.

Now, a given distribution of molecules has an energy associated with it which can be written in the form

$$H = \sum_i \left[ \left( \frac{p_{x_i}^2}{2m} + \frac{p_{y_i}^2}{2m} + \frac{p_{z_i}^2}{2m} \right) + \Phi \right] \tag{6.5}$$

In equation (6.5), $p_{x_i}^2/2m$ is the kinetic energy of the $i$th molecule due to its component of momentum in the $x$ direction $p_{x_i}$ and so on. The term $\Phi$ represents the potential energy of the $i$th molecule due to its interaction with all the other molecules. According to statistical mechanics the probability that a system of molecules has a given position and momentum distribution is proportional to $\exp\left(-H/kT\right)$ and the actual probability that the distribution is $f_N \, dV_N \, dP_N$ is given by

$$f_N \, dV_N \, dP_N = \frac{\exp\left(-H/kT\right) \, dV_N \, dP_N}{\displaystyle\int_{6N} \exp\left(-H/kT\right) \, dV_N \, dP_N} \tag{6.6}$$

The denominator is a normalization factor included to account for the fact that if the probabilities for all the possible distributions were added up, the total is 1, i.e. the actual distribution must correspond to one of the possible ones. The integration is over all the momentum and position co-ordinates, and therefore the evaluation involves 6 N integrations. Equation 6.6 is a fundamental relation, the evaluation of which allows in principle all the thermodyanamic properties of a system to be calculated. The internal energy for example, is just the average value of the energy function $H$,

$$U = \bar{H} = \int H \cdot f_N \, dV_N \, dP_N \qquad (6.7)$$

and similarly, the average of the Virial of the intermolecular forces

$$\sum_{\text{pairs}} r_{ij} \cdot Z(r_{ij})$$

gives via equation (6.3), the ordinary equation of state.

It is the evaluation of the configurational integrals that forms the major problem in the statistical mechanics of fluids. This becomes evident if we attempt to integrate the denominator in equation (6.6). As a start, the exponential term may be split into two factors:

$$\exp \left[ (p_{x_1} \ldots p_{z_N})/2mkT \right] \cdot \exp \left[ \phi_{1,2} \ldots \phi_{N,\,N-1} \right]$$

Integrating the $3N$ components of momentum is not difficult since each integral corresponds to a standard form. The exact result is

$$(2\pi mkT)^{3N/2}$$

However, the second factor cannot be integrated as it stands because each component is a function of more than one variable. This is the major problem that has resulted in the relative retardation of the theory of fluids. Some of the attempts which have been made to avoid or overcome this obstacle to progress are discussed in the next few sections.

## 6.2. The radial distribution function

Consider a typical molecule within the liquid. The number of other molecules that lie within a spherical shell between $r$ and $r + dr$ from the chosen molecule is

$$\rho(r) 4\pi r^2 \, dr$$

where $\rho(r)$ is the radial distribution function (see § 2.2). If the potential between pairs of molecules is of the form $\phi(r)$, then the potential energy that exists between the molecule and others lying within the shell is

$$\phi(r)\rho(r)4\pi r^2 \, dr$$

The total potential energy of the liquid is therefore

$$\Phi = \frac{N}{2} \int_0^\infty \phi(r)\rho(r)4\pi r^2 \, dr$$

Note that a factor $N/2$ rather than $N$ applies because otherwise each interaction would be counted twice, since $\phi(r_{ij}) = \phi(r_{ji})$. The total internal energy of the liquid $U$ is the sum of the potential energy and the kinetic energy, and for a monatomic liquid such as liquid argon

$$U = 3NkT/2 + \Phi$$

The equation of state can be obtained using the Virial Theorem (equation (6.3)). The force $Z(r_{ij})$ acting between the $i$th and $j$th molecule is

$$Z(r_{ij}) = -\,\mathrm{d}\phi(r_{ij})/\mathrm{d}r$$

Therefore the contribution to the virial term from molecules lying within a spherical shell $r$ to $r + \mathrm{d}r$ distant from the reference molecule is

$$-\frac{1}{3}r[\mathrm{d}\rho(r)/\mathrm{d}r]4\pi r^2 \rho(r)\,\mathrm{d}r$$

Integrating over the entire liquid,

$$pV = NkT - \frac{N}{6}\int_0^\infty \mathrm{d}\phi(r)/\mathrm{d}r \,.\, \rho(r)\,.\, 4\pi r^3\,\mathrm{d}r \qquad (6.7)$$

At first sight, equation (6.7) appears to provide a valuable method for determining the equation of state or alternatively, of investigating the potential function $\phi(r)$, because $\rho(r)$ may be measured experimentally by either neutron or X-ray diffraction. Unfortunately, however, it is not possible to determine $\rho(r)$ with sufficient accuracy at present for this to be the case. The results of some recent measurements on liquid argon are shown in fig. 6.1. As can be seen, the curves are relatively insensitive to a quite considerable variation in the density.

The number of molecules lying within various shells may be deduced by estimating the area between $r$ and $r + \mathrm{d}r$ on figures such as 6.1. The number of molecules that may be regarded as effectively nearest neighbours may also be found by estimating the area under the first peak (fig. 6.2). This is called the first co-ordination number. Whereas in solid argon, each molecule has twelve nearest neighbours, the co-ordination number in liquid argon ranges from about 10 at the triple point to $\sim 1$ at the lower densities ($\sim 4$ at the critical point). One feature that emerges from the X-ray investigation is that the co-ordination number appears to vary very little with temperature (fig. 6.3).

Several attempts have been made to solve equation 6.7 using various methods to split the potential term $\mathrm{d}\phi(r)/\mathrm{d}r$ into convenient groups of terms, each a function of one variable only. At a relatively low density, approximations using series have been successful, but at typical liquid densities such methods fail. M. Born and H. S. Green made some progress by considering the change in the pair distribution function $n_2(1,2)$, when one of the molecules is displaced by a small amount. (The pair distribution function $n_2(1,2)$ is the probability of finding molecule 1 at $x_1$, $y_1$, $z_1$ and at the same time molecule 2 at $x_2$, $y_2$, $z_2$.) Unfortunately, their derived expression contained triplet terms, i.e. three molecule distribution functions $n_3(1, 2, 3)$ and these could not be evaluated exactly.

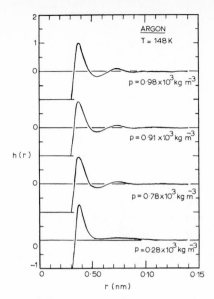

Fig. 6.1.   The radial distribution function of argon $h(r) = g(r) - 1$ at $148 \cdot 2$ K for four different densities (P. J. Mikolaj and C. J. Pings). $[g(r) = \rho(r)/4\pi r^2,$ where $\rho(r)\mathrm{d}r$ represents the probability of finding a molecule at a distance between $r$ and $r + \mathrm{d}r$ from the centre of a typical molecule in the fluid.]

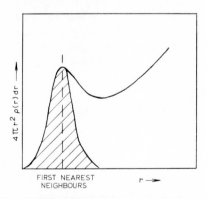

Fig. 6.2.   The first co-ordination number may be deduced by estimating the shaded area under the first peak of a plot of $4\pi r^2 \rho(r)\,\mathrm{d}r$ versus $r$.

A little further progress may be made by taking the Born–Green equations and applying the Kirkwood superposition approximation

$$n_3(1, 2, 3) = [n_2(1, 2) \cdot n_2(2, 3) \cdot n_2(3, 1)]/\rho_0{}^3 \qquad (6.8)$$

to eliminate the triplet terms ($\rho_0$ is the average density in the liquid).

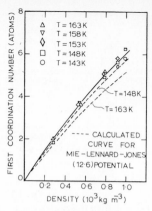

Fig. 6.3. The variation of the first co-ordination number of argon with density. The symbols represent experimental values, the solid line is a quadratic equation fitted to the experimental results and the dashed lines refer to theoretical estimates based on the Mie–Lennard-Jones (6, 12) potential. (P. G. Mikolaj and C. J. Pings.)

J. G. Kirkwood and colleagues have used this approximation to solve equation (6.7) for different types of intermolecular potential, including the Mie–Lennard-Jones (12, 6) form. At lower densities the results agree quite well with experimental data (see Table 6.1), but at densities approaching the solid value the theory breaks down. This is hardly surprising since it is now well established that ' many-body ' effects are important in a liquid and the use of an approximation such as equation (6.8), which eliminates all forces other than pair interactions must therefore lead to erroneous conclusions.

|  | $p^* = \dfrac{p\sigma^3}{\epsilon}$ | $V^* = \left(\dfrac{V}{N\sigma^3}\right)$ | $T^* = \dfrac{kT}{\epsilon}$ | $\dfrac{RT}{pV}$ |
|---|---|---|---|---|
| Calculated | 0·147 | 2·89 | 1·48 | 3·48 |
| Experimental | 0·116 | 3·14 | 1·25 | 3·43 |

Table 6.1. Comparison of critical properties of argon with those calculated by J. G. Kirkwood *et al.* using equation (6.7) with a Mie–Lennard-Jones (6, 12) potential. ($p^*$, $V^*$ and $T^*$ are reduced co-ordinates: $\sigma$ and $\epsilon$ are constants in (6, 12) potential, $k$ is Boltzmann's constant.)

### 6.3. *Partition function method—cell theory*

Another group of investigators have taken what might be called the ' partition function ' approach to the liquid problems. It may formally be shown in statistical mechanics that the free energy $F$ of a system of monatomic molecules is given by

$$F = -kT \ln Z = -kT \ln [(1/h^{3N}N!) \int_{6N} \exp(-H/kT) \,.\, \mathrm{d}V_N \, \mathrm{d}P_N]$$

(6.9)

where $Z$ is the partition function. The term $1/h^{3N}$ is included as a correction required by quantum theory—in calculations on classical systems such as liquid argon, it disappears during the computation. The factor $N! = N(N-1) \ldots 1$ is required to account for the fact that in practice molecules are indistinguishable, i.e. a state in which molecule 1 is at $x_1, y_1, z_1$ and molecules 2 at $x_2, y_2, z_2$ cannot be distinguished from the state in which the two molecules are interchanged.

Exactly the same difficulty arises as was encountered in the previous section when attempts are made to evaluate the partition function. The $3N$ momentum components readily integrate but the $3N$ configurational integrals defy solution. An approach that has been used in an attempt to overcome this obstacle is the cell model. In its most simple form the liquid is considered to consist of a large number of cells, each one occupied by a molecule. Each molecule can move freely about a cell between walls formed by its nearest neighbours (fig. 6.4($a$)). If the molecular diameter is $\sigma$ and the spacing between neighbours is $d$, then the volume of a cell is approximately $4\pi(d-\sigma)^3/3$. Each individual molecule is treated as an independent thermodynamic system, hence if the configurational energy can be evaluated for a single molecule, the total energy of the system is this value multiplied by $N$.

There have been many computations based on the cell model. They differ mainly in the manner in which $\phi(r)$ is assumed to vary within the cell. The easiest situation is one in which the molecule is assumed to be sitting at the bottom of a ' square well ' potential (see fig. 6.4($b$)), in which the potential is assumed to have a constant value throughout the cell, and to rise to infinity at the walls. This must lead to un-realistic answers however, because it assumes that the molecules are hard spheres whereas they are slightly ' soft ', and attractive forces are totally neglected. The more recent computations (Lennard-Jones–Devonshire theory) use a Mie–Lennard-Jones (12, 6) potential. The results of some calculations on liquid argon near the triple point are compared with experimental data for the liquid and solid in Table 6.2. The somewhat surprising feature of the model is that it appears to provide a better description of a solid than it does of a liquid.

There are at least three valid reasons as to why this should be the case. Firstly, using a lattice-like model introduces long-range order into a liquid, whereas X-ray and neutron scattering measurements indicate that only short-range order exists. Secondly, because each molecule is considered as a separate thermodynamic entity, the possibility of co-operative forces or of correlations between molecules in neighbouring cells is ruled out. Thirdly, the rigid walls prevent the interchange of

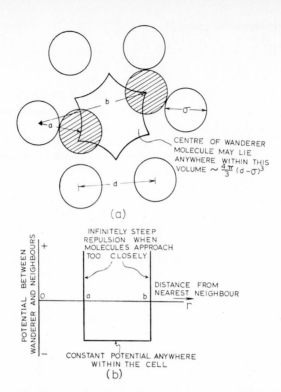

Fig. 6.4. (a) Cell model for a liquid, in which each molecule is considered to be trapped in a cage by its neighbours. (b) 'Square well' intermolecular potential.

|  |  | $\dfrac{\text{Volume}}{N\sigma^3}$ | $\dfrac{U}{N\epsilon}$ | $\dfrac{S}{Nk}$ | $\dfrac{C_v}{Nk}$ |
|---|---|---|---|---|---|
| Experimental | solid | 1·035 | −7·14 | −5·33 | 1·41 |
| | liquid | 1·186 | −5·96 | −3·64 | 0·85 |
| L.J.D. theory | | 1·037 | −7·32 | −5·51 | 1·11 |

Table 6.2. Comparison of properties of liquid and solid argon at the triple point with the values predicted by the Lennard-Jones–Devonshire (L.J.D.) theory.

molecules between cells. In statistical mechanical terms, this results in some of the possible configurations being missing from the averaging process.

A related model is the lattice gas or hole model. Here the liquid is again considered to be divided up into a large number of imaginary cells, but in this case some of the cells are occupied while others are empty. Each molecule thus finds itself surrounded by some other molecules and some holes. The detailed mathematical arguments are basically similar to those used in the cell model. It has recently received considerable attention because of the realization that some important magnetic models are basically equivalent. Thus the Ising model of a ferromagnet is identical with the lattice gas model of a fluid. Theoretical progress made in the theory of magnetism therefore may result in an equivalent advance in the liquid state, and vice versa. This aspect will be pursued a little further in Chapter 7.

### 6.4. *Computer calculations*

One of the chief shortcomings of models such as the cell model is that the molecules are static. The molecules in a real fluid are in ceaseless motion, continuously changing their positions. Only for periods $\sim 10^{-15}$ s can a liquid be regarded as static. With the advent of the high-speed digital computer it has become possible to simulate this behaviour for a small number of molecules ($\sim 100$).

Consider a small number of molecules contained in a box (fig. 6.5).

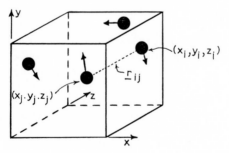

Fig. 6.5. Molecules in a box may be used in computer calculations.

The position of each one may be specified by three co-ordinates $x_i, y_i, z_i$. The complete set of co-ordinates then corresponds to a particular configuration of the system. By allowing one of the molecules to be displaced a random amount a new configuration is generated. This process is continued one molecule at a time until a large number of different configurations have occurred. After each move, the computer calculates the distance $r_{ij}$ between each pair of molecules and hence the total potential of the system $\Phi = \sum_{\text{pairs}} \phi(r_{ij})$. The probability of getting a configuration of energy $\Phi$ is proportional to the Boltzmann factor $\exp(-\Phi/kT)$. Averaging the $\Phi$ obtained for a large number of configurations gives the potential energy component of the internal energy. Similarly, the average virial obtained from a large number of configurations $\frac{1}{3} \sum_{\text{pairs}} r_{ij} \cdot Z(r_{ij})$ allows the equation of state to be determined.

The *Monte Carlo* method uses the computer's facility for generating random numbers. First of all, one of the molecules is chosen at random. It is then assumed to have moved a random distance within certain limits—again set by the computer. If the move takes it outside the box, then it is deemed to have reappeared on the other side (fig. 6.6),

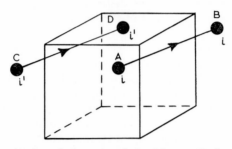

Fig. 6.6. 'Ghosting' technique used in Monte Carlo calculations. As molecule $i$ moves out of the box ($A \rightarrow B$), its ghost $i'$ is deemed to have entered ($C \rightarrow D$) and is used in subsequent calculations.

and this ' ghost ' is used for further moves. There is a special procedure for cases in which a move brings a molecule too close to another one. A move which lands a molecule on top of another molecule is rejected outright and the molecule is returned to its original position. This is equivalent to an elastic collision. Further, only a certain proportion of those moves which bring a molecule close to another one are allowed. The appropriate configurational properties are calculated at each stage.

In the *molecular dynamics method* the positions and velocities of a small number of molecules contained within a box are specified at $t=0$. It is assumed that each molecule moves in a straight line until it collides with another one after which the motions of the two are determined by Newton's laws. Molecular interaction is thus reduced to a rapid sequence of two-body collisions. The Monte Carlo ghosting technique is used when a molecule passes through a wall of the box. After each collision the computer finds the new velocities and directions of the molecules concerned. By analysing the motion of all the molecules, the computer is able to determine those molecules which are involved in the next collision. Again at each stage the appropriate configurational properties are calculated.

In both the Monte Carlo method and the molecular dyanamics method the accuracy of the results is governed partially by the number of molecules and the size of the box (with its surface effects), but more importantly by the total number of configurations that are generated. At least 50 000 to 100 000 different configurations are required if the averaging process is to satisfy the needs of statistical mechanics. Even with a high-speed computer this takes a long time. For example, a Monte Carlo calculation on a system of 108 molecules interacting with a Mie–Lennard-Jones potential requires 1 hour on the University of London Atlas computer to generate 168 000 configurations. This is equivalent to just *one* data point!

The output from molecular dynamical computations may be fed from the computer on to a cathode ray oscilloscope. In this way the motions of individual molecules may be observed visually. By photographing, a record of the molecular motion over a period of time is obtained. Studies of this type were pioneered by B. Alder. Some typical results for a molecular system at four different densities are shown in fig. 6.7. The packings correspond to : (a) solid phase;

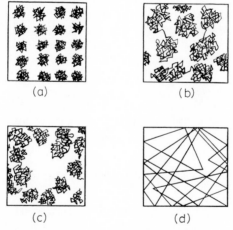

Fig. 6.7. Molecular dynamics of molecules in a box. (*a*) Solid density—motion about lattice site. (*b*) Liquid—oscillation in cell but with occasional interchange. (*c*) Liquid–vapour—bubbles of vapour formed within liquid. (*d*) Gas—collisions mainly with walls but with occasional intermolecular collisions.

(b) liquid phase; (c) liquid–vapour phase; and (d) gas phase. In (a) the molecules vibrate about fixed lattice sites. In (b), the motion is largely about fixed positions but is more vigorous, with occasional interchanges. Bubbles of vapour appear in the liquid (c) at slightly lower density, and motion is much more vigorous in the gas (d). ' Collisions ' with the walls increase considerably as we progress from

(a) to (d), thus indicating, as one would expect, that the pressure exerted by a gas on its container is greater than the bombardment pressure *for the same number of molecules* in the liquid phase or the solid phase.

## 6.5. *Experiments with static models*

Dynamic calculations using the Monte Carlo or molecular dynamic techniques require a great deal of expensive computing time. There are, however, some experiments with extremely simple apparatus that give considerable insight into the nature of the liquid state. Those described here have largely been pioneered by J. D. Bernal in England and G. D. Scott in Canada.

Suppose that a number of small steel spheres ($\sim 3$ mm in diameter) are dropped into a glass measuring cylinder. The volume that they occupy may be read from the scale. Shaking or tapping the cylinder causes a small reduction in volume. By pouring wax into the cylinder the spheres may be fixed in their positions. Subsequent examination of the assembly and the careful removal of the spheres one by one, allows both the number of points of contact and the positions of each sphere in a convenient co-ordinate reference frame to be determined (fig. 6.8). The wax can be removed by scraping and the position of

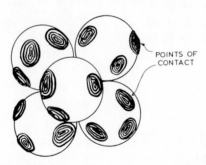

Fig. 6.8. Section of assembly of spheres showing how points of contact are seen by wax imprints.

each sphere measured before removal using a travelling microscope fitted with two horizontal scales and a vertical scale. In this way the number of nearest neighbours (the first co-ordination number) and the radial distribution function can be determined.

The results of such experiments suggest that the number of nearest neighbours varies between about four and eleven (spheres close packed as in a solid have twelve nearest neighbours), and the density is about 90% of the maximum. Radial distribution functions calculated by this method are shown in fig. 6.9, compared with one actually measured $\rho(r)$ for liquid argon. The agreement is most impressive, although

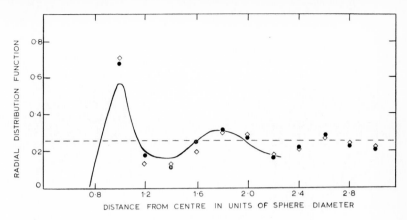

Fig. 6.9. Radial distribution function $g(r)$ for liquid argon compared with distribution estimated from steel sphere model. ● Bernal, ◇ Scott.

it should be remembered from § 6.2 that the radial distribution function is a relatively insensitive test of models.

Another intriguing geometrical property was discovered by Bernal in the course of some experiments with Plasticine spheres. A number of Plasticine spheres, dusted with talcum powder so that they would not stick together, were placed in a football bladder. After the residual air had been removed, the bladder was then compressed until the Plasticine formed a compact mass. On removing the Plasticine and separating it into individual blocks, Bernal found that these had become irregular polyhedra. The average number of faces per polyhedron was 13·6 and the most common number of sides to each face was five. The value of five was significant from the crystallographic viewpoint, because it is well established that although molecules in crystals may be arranged with two, three, four or six-fold symmetry, close-packing (so as to leave no gaps) with five-fold symmetry is impossible (fig. 6.10). As Bernal points out—' it is like trying to pave a floor with five sided tiles '.

These studies have the merits of being simple and inexpensive. They offer intriguing evidence that the structure of a liquid may be determined at least to some extent by geometrical factors. But it still remains difficult to put them on a proper quantitative basis. As static models they may be regarded as representing instantaneous snapshots of molecular configuration in a liquid with an exposure of about $10^{-15}$ s. To some extent their intrinsic appeal has been overshadowed by the recent successes of the dynamic computing methods.

### 6.6. Comparison of liquid state theories

Before concluding this examination of liquid state properties, it is worth comparing how well the various approaches describe the proper-

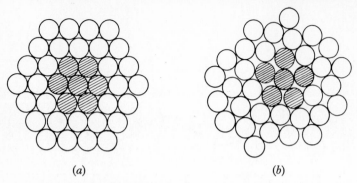

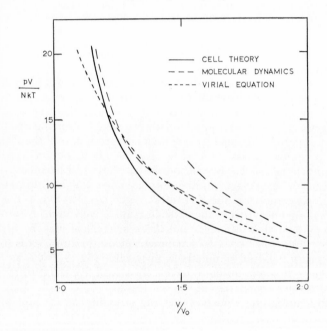

Fig. 6.10. Close-packing is possible with (a) sixfold but not (b) five-fold symmetry in crystals.

Fig. 6.11. Comparison of the results of hard-sphere calculations using different theoretical approaches.

ties of a real fluid such as liquid argon. To do this, the calculations can be placed in two categories, those using hard spheres (which means a potential with a sharp cut-off) and those using the more realistic Mie–Lennard-Jones (12, 6) potential. Some results of hard-sphere calculations are shown in fig. 6.11. It can be seen that cell theory agrees with molecular dynamics only at high densities. This is what

94

would be expected, since the cell theory would be expected to provide a better description at near-solid densities, and molecular dynamics to be equally valid for all packing. One interesting feature that emerges from both Monte Carlo and molecular dynamics calculations is that two separate curves are possible, the one obtained depending on the initial density of the system. It is found that if the computation is started at a high density, as the box size is increased, the lattice structure persists even down to low densities. On the other hand, if the initial size of the box is large, long range order never appears to set in, even when the density becomes high.

One would expect calculations based on the Mie–Lennard-Jones potential to provide a more accurate description of the properties of liquid argon. The results of some computations using the (6, 12) form are shown in fig. 6.12. Here again the Monte Carlo calculations lie

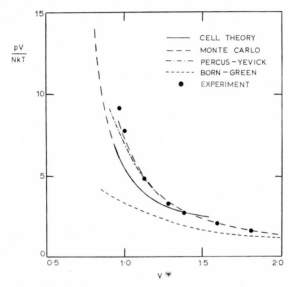

Fig. 6.12. Comparison of the results of theoretical calculations using Mie–Lennard-Jones (6, 12) potential with experimental values at $T^* = -kT/\epsilon = 2\cdot74\,(\sim 2T_c)$. $[V^* = V/N\,\sigma^3.]$

on two curves, which may be identified as two distinct phases. The portion corresponding to the ordered phase joins up smoothly with the predictions of the cell model, reinforcing the view that cell theories provide a better description of a solid than they do of a liquid. It seems that dynamic computing methods provide the best description of the liquid state and it is to be expected that when calculations with larger assemblies of molecules are carried out, agreement with experimental data will become even better.

Also shown in fig. 6.12 and in very good agreement with experiment are the results of calculations based on a theory originated by J. K. Percus and G. J. Yevick. Percus and Yevick argued that if the spectrum of a liquid was known then its properties could be calculated, analogous to the way in which they are computed for a solid. It has already been pointed out that the greatest obstacle to evaluating the integrals in equations such as equation (6.6) lies in separating the potential energy terms into components which depend on the co-ordinates of single molecules only. The Percus–Yevick approach provides a means of overcoming this difficulty. Instead of defining the positions of molecules in terms of their individual position co-ordinates $x_1, y_1, z_1 \ldots z_N$, these are replaced by ' collective variables ', each of which is a function of all the co-ordinates. On substitution of these in the expression for the potential energy it is found that terms may be separated into groups, each a function of *one* co-ordinate, and hence the integration can be done. This description is somewhat over-simplified. Some assumptions have to be made which appear to be more valid than those used in earlier models. However, the predictions do appear to be in excellent agreement with the results of both molecular dynamics and of experiment and this is probably sufficient justification to take the theory very seriously!

This chapter has been confined to a discussion of the equilibrium properties of liquids. The theory of transport phenomena is in an even more rudimentary state. There is still an enormous amount of work to be done, both theoretical and experimental, before we can begin to think that the liquid state is understood. On the experimental side, accurate measurements of nearly every property over as wide a range of thermal states as possible are required, particularly on the simple systems represented by the liquid inert gases. It would be particularly valuable to have a systematic series of measurements of related properties carried out on say liquid argon, at states for which X-ray or neutron diffraction scattering data are available. Only too often in the past investigations have been too independent of each other and have not been sufficiently systematic to be of great value. Measurements along isochores (constant volume) for example, allow the specific influence of temperature on a property to be determined. On the theoretical side, integral equations such as provided by the Percus–Yevick approach will have to be developed further and a whole range of non-equilibrium properties investigated. To repeat, although enormous advances in the understanding of liquid state properties have taken place within the last two decades, there is a great deal of work still to be done!

# CHAPTER 7
## critical phenomena

### 7.1. *Introduction*

ONE of the fascinating features of science is the manner in which topics which appear to be exhausted of interest spring to life once more as a result of new and sometimes unexpected discoveries. The study of the inert gases themselves is one example. A subject that is currently exciting a great deal of interest is the study of ' critical phenomena '. Although this book is about inert gases, and therefore we are mainly concerned with gas–liquid critical points, the development of the subject is inextricably linked with the development of the theory of magnetism and so some discussion of magnetic properties will be included in this chapter where appropriate.

It is now almost exactly a hundred years ago since T. Andrews presented to the Royal Society a report of his observations of the behaviour of carbon dioxide gas under pressure. He explained that whereas he found it possible to liquefy the gas at temperatures up to 304 K by increasing the pressure at constant temperature, above this ' critical point ' liquefaction did not appear to take place. Before long, similar observations for other gases were reported, and it became clear that this behaviour was general, and shown by most substances.

Within a few years of Andrews' report to the Royal Society, van der Waals had proposed his equation of state for a real gas (equation 6.1) which took into account attractive forces between molecules and the finite volume that they occupy. This semi-empirical equation, together with a further assumption to be discussed in the next section, gives a remarkable qualitative description of the behaviour of a fluid in the gaseous and liquid phases, and also predicts the existence of a critical point. At the turn of the century, rapid progress was also being made in another and seemingly unrelated branch of physics. In 1895, the existence of Curie points in ferromagnetic materials was established. When a magnetic field $H$ is applied to a ferromagnet and then reduced to zero the material remains partially magnetized unless the temperature is higher than a transition temperature, which is characteristic of the material, and called the Curie point ($T_c$). The Curie point appears to play a role in magnetism very similar to that of critical point in a fluid. For example, above $T_c$, the compressibility of a fluid (van der Waals) and the susceptibility of a ferromagnet (Curie–Weiss) are both proportional to $(T - T_c)^{-1}$. A detailed examination demonstrates that this analogy is not merely superficial, and it is found that appropriate magnetic and thermal properties of the two systems vary in a strikingly similar manner as the transition temperatures are approached. For example, the specific heat capacity of a fluid at constant pressure is found to vary with temperature in exactly the same way, within experimental error, as the specific heat capacity of a ferromagnet in a constant magnetic field: so pressure in the first system is analogous to magnetic field in the second. Because of these similarities, it is therefore not surprising that we also find much common ground in the theoretical approaches that have been proposed to describe these systems. Weiss explained the residual magnetization of a ferromagnet in zero field in terms of an ' internal field '. The assumptions and predictions of this theory correspond remarkably to those for a van der Waals fluid. At a more sophisticated level, the Ising model of a ferromagnet is equivalent, in terms of statistical mechanics, to the lattice gas model of a fluid. In the Ising model, the magnetic ions are represented by magnetic spins, some of which point in one direction and the others in the opposite direction. In the lattice gas model, the fluid is considered to be divided into cells, some of which are occupied by molecules and others of which are empty.

The recent revival of interest in the fluid critical region has been due to a combination of factors, some theoretical and some experimental. Until recently, it proved to be extremely difficult to improve much on the semi-empirical approach of van der Waals. For whereas both a low density gas and a solid are amenable to statistical mechanical analysis using exact (or plausible approximate) methods, a dense gas or a fluid poses problems that are mathematically intractable. These have been discussed in Chapter 6. Recently, however, some progress has been made in evaluating the configurational integrals. The behaviour of statistical functions in the region of phase transitions have also been investigated. In thermodynamic terms, it is found that critical points are more complicated than was originally appreciated. For example, the simple and seemingly innocuous assumption that one may regard the critical point as an ordinary thermodynamic state and treat deviations from it by simple series-expansion methods is now known to be invalid and misleading.

The important results for the exact solution of the two dimensional Ising model of a ferromagnet obtained by L. Onsager in 1944, may be translated simply and directly into the equivalent model in fluid physics, the two-dimensional lattice gas. Useful cross-fertilization of this kind plus corresponding progress in experimental techniques have combined to lead to rapid advance in an understanding of the subject. Highly accurate specific heat determinations in which $T_c$ has been approached to within $10^{-4}$ K, and sophisticated magnetic experiments, have established beyond doubt that the simple approach behind the van der Waals equation and the Curie–Weiss law (magnetic susceptibility $\propto (T - T_c)^{-1}$)

is deficient. However, there are many important experiments still to be done and here once again, because the inert gases correspond to simple models, they provide ideal systems with which to test theoretical predictions. The critical properties of the inert gases are summarized in Table 7.1.

| Gas | Critical temperature (K) | Critical pressure (kN m$^{-2}$) | Critical density (kg m$^{-3}$) |
|---|---|---|---|
| $^3$He | 3·3 | 116 | — |
| $^4$He | 5·3 | 229 | 69·3 |
| Ne | 44·5 | 2730 | 484 |
| Ar | 150·9 | 4900 | 536 |
| Kr | 209·4 | 5510 | 908 |
| Xe | 289·8 | 5850 | 1100 |
| Rn | 378·2 | 6290 | — |

Table 7.1. Critical properties of the inert gases.

## 7.2. *Liquid-vapour critical point*

Consider a closed system in which a substance is confined to a vessel such that the temperature, pressure and volume may be varied and also measured, so that a $p$–$V$ phase diagram similar to that shown in fig. 7.1 may be obtained (compare this with fig. 2.11). By following a thermodynamic path that passes above the critical temperature $T_c$ (e.g. $AB$) it is possible to change the system from a gas ($A$) to a liquid ($B$), without apparent discontinuity in the physical properties, or the Helmholtz free energy $F$ (see Appendix), or first-partial derivatives of the free energy (see § 6.1). The work done in carrying out the compression depends on the temperature $T$. At critical volume ($V_c$) the compressibility, $k_T = -(\partial V/\partial p)_T/V$ increases rapidly as $T$ tends towards $T_c$. This observation may conveniently be expressed as

$$k_T \to \infty \quad \text{as} \quad T \to T_c^+ (V = V_c) \tag{7.1}$$

where $T_c^+$ denotes approach to $T_c$ from above.

Now consider the path $CD$. As the gas is compressed, the density increases until it reaches a value $\rho_v$ at which the pressure is equal to the saturated equilibrium vapour-pressure for that particular temperature ($E$). At this point the pressure remains constant, and further compression will cause condensation of part of the gas to a liquid of density

99

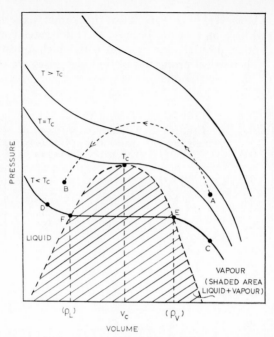

Fig. 7.1. Pressure–volume phase diagram for a one-component fluid in the region of the critical point. (The two-phase region is shaded.)

$\rho_l$. At $F$ the gas is completely converted to the liquid. In the two-phase region, $EF$, the density difference $(\rho_l - \rho_v)$ depends only on the temperature $T$, and it is observed that

$$(\rho_l - \rho_v) \to 0 \quad \text{as} \quad T \to T_c^- \tag{7.2}$$

The relations described by 7.1 and 7.2 serve jointly to define the critical point.

In addition to these properties there is a striking thermal anomaly associated with the critical region. It is found that the specific heat capacity at critical volume tends to infinity as $T \to T_c^{\pm}$. Whether or not the value would actually reach infinity at $T_c$, is, of course, impossible to determine experimentally. Certainly, recent very careful and accurate measurements on argon (fig. 7.2), and helium, by Voronel and Russian co-workers indicate that the value reached is at least 20 times greater than the expected configurational specific heat at that density.

Another feature characteristic of the critical region is the very strong light scattering that is observed as the critical point is approached. Light is scattered by fluctuations in the dielectric constant which vary with position and time. These in turn arise from fluctuations in the density of the fluid, which also govern the compressibility. As $T \to T_c^+$,

100

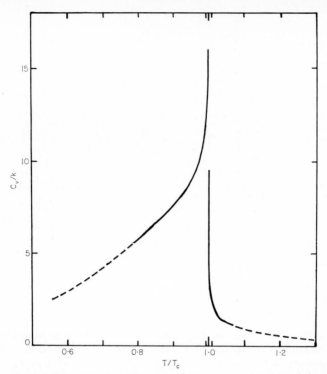

Fig. 7.2. Molar heat capacity of fluid argon near the critical density (Voronel 1965).

the compressibility $k_T \to \infty$ and this is accompanied by a very dramatic increase in scattering. Close to $T_c$ ($\Delta T \approx 0.05$ K), the fluid becomes completely opaque. Physically, one might imagine that as $T_c$ is approached large clusters, or groups of molecules, occur with increasing frequency and the strong scattering is due to the increase in size and coherence of these clusters.

## 7.3. *The law of corresponding states—critical indices*

When the densities of the liquid and vapour in equilibrium along the coexistence curve are measured for a variety of substances, it is found that the results for density and temperature, when normalized by dividing by their values at $T_c$, are practically identical. This may be seen by plotting the results on a single graph (fig. 7.3). Most of the observed scatter in fig. 7.3 is in fact probably due to experimental error rather than to genuine differences in behaviour. This is the principle of the law of corresponding states—simple substances exhibit identical behaviour when their properties are described in terms of reduced parameters.

101

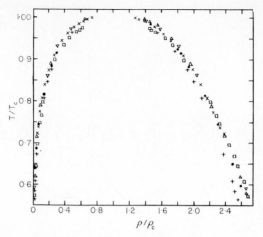

Fig. 7.3. Density coexistence curve for different substances, demonstrating the law of corresponding states: + neon, ● argon, × xenon, △ nitrogen, ▽ oxygen, □ carbon monoxide. Most of the scatter is probably due to experimental error rather than to fundamental difference in behaviour (Guggenheim 1945).

The principle works well in practice for a wide range of substances. It is therefore very convenient when making comparisons between different experiments and between theory and experiment to express the behaviour in terms of the critical parameters $p_c$, $V_c$, $T_c$. It is particularly useful from a thermodynamic viewpoint to examine the variation of properties along the coexistence curve, along the critical isochore $(V = V_c)$, and along the critical isotherm. It has been found that these properties may usually be described quite accurately by expressions of the form

$$X = A(T - T_c)^B$$

where $A$ is a parameter characteristic of each particular substance and $B$ is an index common to all substances. For example, the difference in density between a liquid and a vapour in equilibrium at a temperature below $T_c$ may be expressed as

$$\rho_l - \rho_v = A(T_c - T)^\beta$$

where $\beta \approx 0.35$. Similarly the variation with temperature of the compressibility of a fluid at the critical value $V = V_c$, $(T > T_c)$, is given by

$$k_T = D(T - T_c)^\gamma$$

where $D$ is a constant for a given fluid and $\gamma \approx -1$. Critical indices such as $\beta$ and $\gamma$ are thought to have values that are independent of the substance studied. It is possible, however, that in practice they might vary with the temperature range of $(T - T_c)$ studied, and for this reason they are generally defined in terms of their limiting value as $T \to T_c$, for

102

example

$$\beta = \text{limit }_{T \to T_c^-} \left[ \ln \left( \rho_l - \rho_v \right) / \ln \left( T_c - T \right) \right]$$

Some indices that are important and in common use are defined in Table 7.2.

| Property | Index | Definition | Prediction of classical theory |
|---|---|---|---|
| $C_v$ | $\alpha^+$ | $\rho = \rho_c,\ T \to T_c^+$ | 0 (discontinuity) |
| | $\alpha^-$ | coexistence, $T \to T_c^-$ | 0 (discontinuity) |
| $(\rho_l - \rho_v)$ | $\beta$ | coexistence, $T \to T_c^-$ | $\frac{1}{2}$ |
| $(\partial p / \partial V)_T$ | $\gamma^+$ | $\rho = \rho_c,\ T \to T_c^-$ | 1 |
| | $\gamma^-$ | coexistence, $T \to T_c^-$ | 1 |
| $p - p_c \approx |V - V_c|$ | $\delta$ | $\rho \to \rho_c,\ T = T_c$ | 3 |

Table 7.2.   Definition of some critical exponents, together with the predictions of classical (van der Waals) theory.

## 7.4. *Classical theoretical models*

At first sight, the concept of the 'internal field' introduced by Weiss in 1907 to describe the behaviour of ferromagnetic materials in the region of the Curie point appears to have nothing in common with van der Waals' approach to a fluid. However, a closer examination shows that both approaches share two important defects, namely they do not account for the fluctuation phenomena which occur in the critical region, and are a poor approximation for systems in which the significant interactions are short range.

The predictions of these classical 'phenomenological' theories may be summarized as follows (see Table 7.2). At the critical point the specific heat makes a finite jump and then decreases again. The size of the discontinuity for a van der Waals fluid at critical volume is

$$\Delta C_v = C_V - \frac{3R}{2} = 0 \text{ if } T > T_c,$$

otherwise

$$= \frac{9}{2} R \left[ 1 - \frac{28}{25} \frac{T_c - T}{T_c} + \ldots \right]$$

whereas for a ferromagnet, magnetized to its critical value,

$$\Delta C_m = 0 \text{ if } T > T_c,$$

otherwise

$$= \frac{5}{2} R \left[ 1 - \frac{13}{5} \frac{T_c - T}{T_c} + \ldots \right]$$

103

The coexistence curve in both cases is parabolic in the region of the critical point (i.e. $\beta = \frac{1}{2}$). Also, as $T \to T_c^+$, the compressibility of a fluid or susceptibility of a ferromagnet becomes infinite, since both are proportional to $1/(T - T_c)$.

In both cases the properties are obtained via a Taylor expansion, in which the appropriate free energy is expressed in terms of the order parameter, e.g. density or magnetization. (In fact, it appears that the critical indices are relatively insensitive to the exact form of the equation used.) It is now firmly established however, that the critical point is mathematically non-analytic, in the sense that it is not possible to carry out an expansion that is convergent in every neighbourhood of the critical point, except in the limit of infinitely weak and long-range forces. It is also clear that the interactions between molecules in these systems are essentially short-range, involving at most a few shells of neighbouring atoms. Therefore it is not surprising that the results of experiment do not confirm predictions based on the above assumption (see Table 7.3).

| Index | Classical theory | Ising $D=2$ | Ising $D=3$ | Heisenberg $D=3$ | Experiment | |
|---|---|---|---|---|---|---|
| | | | | | fluid | ferromagnet |
| $\alpha^+$ | 0 (discontinuity) | 0 (log) | $\frac{1}{8} \pm 0\cdot015$ | $\approx 0(?)$ | $\geqslant 0$ | $\approx 0$ |
| $\alpha^-$ | 0 (discontinuity) | 0 (log) | $\frac{1}{16}(+0\cdot16 -0\cdot035)$ | (?) | $\approx 0$ (log) | $\approx 0$ (log) |
| $\beta$ | $\frac{1}{2}$ | $\frac{1}{8}$ | $\frac{5}{16}(+0\cdot003 -0\cdot006)$ | (?) | $\approx 0\cdot34$ | $\approx 0\cdot33$ |
| $\gamma^+$ | 1 | $1\frac{3}{4}$ | $1\frac{1}{4} \pm 0\cdot003$ | $1\cdot33-1\cdot43$ | $\gtrsim 1\cdot2$ | $\approx 1\cdot35$ |
| $\gamma^-$ | 1 | $1\frac{3}{4}$ | $1\frac{5}{16}(+0\cdot03 -0\cdot05)$ | ? | $\gtrsim 1\cdot2$ | ? |
| $\delta$ | 3 | 15 | $5\frac{1}{5} \pm 0\cdot15$ | ? | $\approx 4\cdot2$ | $\gtrsim 4\cdot2$ |

Table 7.3. A comparison of theoretical predictions for some critical exponents with experimental results for fluids and ferromagnets.

## 7.5. *Exact theories*

The most important advance in the understanding of critical phenomena came in 1944, when Onsager produced the exact solution of the two-dimensional Ising model of a ferromagnet. This assumes short-range forces and allows the possibility of the fluctuations, which are known to play an important role in the critical region. The Ising model is in fact a simplified version of another model, the Heisenberg model.

As has already been mentioned, the magnetic Ising model is equivalent to the lattice gas description of a fluid. In this model the space occupied by the fluid is divided up by a regular space lattice into a large

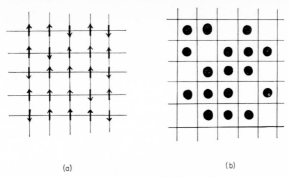

(a)                                    (b)

Fig. 7.4.   (a) Two-dimensional Ising model for a ferromagnet.    (b) Equivalent two-dimensional lattice gas model for a fluid.

number of cells.   Some of the cells are occupied by molecules and others are empty (fig. 7.4(a)).   It is assumed that each molecule is strictly localized to its own cell and double occupancy is specifically prohibited.   Providing that the lattice spacing is small compared with the distance over which the pair potential varies significantly, the configurational integrals in the partition function may be replaced by simplified functions and thus evaluated.   This is because the interactions may be reduced to a simple scheme in which there are only two possible states, depending on whether a cell is occupied or unoccupied.

The analogy with the Ising ferromagnet is quite straightforward. The occupancy of sites corresponds to whether the spins are parallel or anti-parallel, the number of cells is equal to the total number of spins, and the two states which describe nearest neighbour interactions may be applied equally well to either cell occupancy or spin direction.   The density of the fluid is analogous to the magnetization of the lattice, and pressure is analogous to magnetic field, since an increase in pressure will cause more cells to be occupied, and an increase in field will alter the number of spins aligned in a particular direction.   In a more formal treatment this equivalence may be established in terms of statistical mechanics.   In statistical mechanics, partition functions are used to describe the probability that the molecules in a system have a particular configuration (see § 6.3).   The canonical and grand canonical functions are obtained using different statistical approaches to the problem.   It is found that the grand canonical partition function of the lattice gas corresponds to the canonical partition function for the Ising ferromagnet where changes in chemical potential $\mu$ (chemical potential $= \partial G/\partial n$, where $n$ is the molar concentration) correspond to changes in the magnetic field.   This equivalence was first established by Lee and Yang in 1952.   It may be shown also that another statistical representation of a ferromagnet—the Heisenberg model, is equivalent to the 'continuum' model of a fluid.

105

The Ising model in one dimension was proposed in 1925 and although it is in itself a simplified model, the exact solution proved to be difficult. In one dimension no phase change is observed. The two-dimensional case was not solved until 1944, when Onsager succeeded in obtaining an exact solution for the lattice in zero magnetic field. The most significant result of this calculation is that a logarithmic singularity for the specific heat capacity is predicted, contrary to the pole divergence (i.e. $C_v \propto 1/(T - T_c)$) that emerges from phenomenological approaches. Even today, exact solutions for the three-dimensional problem remain elusive. It is known that Onsager's method may not be applied in three dimensions because it relies on a topological property of two-dimensional lattices which is not shared with their three-dimensional counterparts. One is left, therefore, with various mathematical approaches that use series methods, for example, functions called Padé approximants, to obtain approximate answers. The current position is summarized in Table 7.3. Obviously there is considerable progress still to be made. However, the fact that these models embody the important features of short-range forces, and the possibility of fluctuations in the order parameter (density or residual magnetization), both of which are known to contribute to critical phenomena, already suggests that the models are superior to the older phenomenological theories.

The Heisenberg magnet and the continuum fluid models might ultimately give a better description of critical behaviour. However, these are proving to be mathematically intractable. Some progress has been made but exact solutions are in general hard to obtain, particularly for the three-dimensional cases.

## 7.6. *Experiments in the critical region*

Reliable experimental data are difficult to obtain in the critical region largely because of problems of non-equilibrium. This can best be illustrated by examining the results of a classical experiment, the density measurements on xenon by M. A. Weinberger and W. G. Schneider (fig. 7.5($a$)). These were made using two cells, one vertical and of effective height 10 cm, and the other horizontal and of effective height 1 cm. The difference between the results is due to the effects of gravity, i.e. the hydrostatic head is greater in one case than the other. This problem arises because of the rapid increase in the compressibility of a fluid as $T_c$ is approached. To a large extent it may be overcome by examining only a very small horizontal slice of fluid, and making a correction for the effect of the hydrostatic head. The data of Weinberger and Schneider, adjusted for gravity, are shown plotted as $\rho_l - \rho_v$ versus $(1 - T/T_c)^{1/3}$ in fig. 7.5($b$). The experimental points appear to lie on a very reasonable straight line and hence it is easy to conclude that in fact $\beta = 0.33$. However, as Fisher and others have

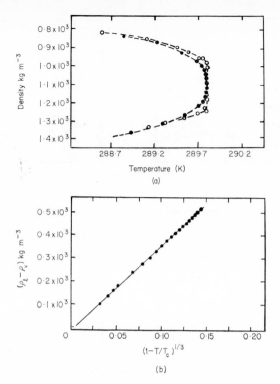

Fig. 7.5. (a) Effect of gravity on density of xenon near $T_c$: ●, cell $10^{-2}$ m high, ○, cell $10^{-1}$ m high. (b) Variation of $(\rho_l - \rho_v)$ for xenon with temperature (Weinberger and Schneider 1952).

pointed out, equally good straight lines may be obtained using quite different values of $\beta$. A more sophisticated numerical analysis of the data leads to the conclusion that $\beta = 0.345 \pm 0.015$ is the best value.

In addition there is the problem of thermal equilibrium. Since the specific heat rises rapidly in the region of $T_c$ one would expect the thermal conductivity also to decrease significantly. (A recent experiment suggests that in fact the thermal conductivity may increase near $T_c$.) These factors combine to make it necessary to wait a long time for the system to reach equilibrium. Very close to $T_c$ periods of up to several days are found to be necessary before a satisfactory steady state is reached. Because of these various difficulties and uncertainties which arise near $T_c$, it is not entirely clear which are the best data to use in order to establish critical indices. Since these are defined as the limits of a property as $T \to T_c$, there are good grounds for attempting to use information taken from as close to $T_c$ as possible. On the other hand, since doubts about equilibrium and other uncertainties are more significant near $T_c$, it is possible to make a convincing case for using

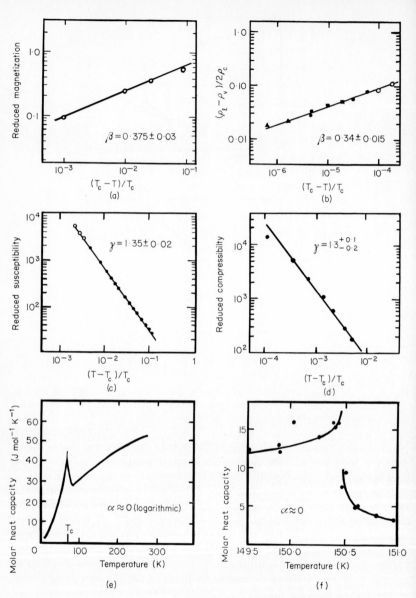

Fig. 7.6. Comparison of typical properties of ferromagnets with the equivalent property of a one-component inert gas fluid. (a) Spontaneous magnetization curve of nickel. (b) Coexistence curve for argon. (c) Reduced susceptibility of nickel. (d) Reduced compressibility of xenon at critical density. (e) Molar heat anomaly in EuO. (f) Molar heat capacity of fluid argon at critical density near $T_c$.

reliable data from as wide a temperature range as possible and then extrapolating rather further to the critical point.

Problems of hysteresis and of equilibrium also occur in magnetic experiments. Undesirable effects may be reduced considerably by using pure single-crystal, single-domain specimens. In addition, a 'shape' correction has to be applied to the field measurements, since the true internal magnetic field will not be identical with the external applied field.

The results of some important determinations of critical indices of inert gas fluids and ferromagnets are compared in fig. 7.6. Note the similarity in the values obtained for the two classes of system.

## 7.7. *Other critical phenomena—$^4$He superfluidity*

Several other 'critical phenomena' have since been established. For example, some binary alloys exhibit an ordering temperature above which long range order of the atoms no longer exists. Antiferromagnets (magnetic materials in which neighbouring spins tend to align in opposite directions) behave in a similar manner, insofar as above the critical temperature (Néel point) the long range ordering of alternate magnetic spins disappears. It is interesting to consider to what extent other transitions, for example, the superfluidity transition in liquid $^4$He, are identical to the above.

The phase diagram of $^4$He has already been shown in Chapter 2 (fig. 2.12). The transition to superfluidity at the $\lambda$ point is a line in the $p$–$T$ plane, rather than a single point, and the specific heat experiments of W. M. Fairbank and others have established to a high degree of accuracy that $\alpha = \alpha^- = 0$ ($\pm 0.03$) over about four decades of $\Delta T / T_c$ and approaching to within $\Delta T / T_c \approx 10^{-6}$ of the transition (fig. 7.7). One runs into difficulties, however, when attempting to define some of the critical indices—$\gamma$, $\gamma^-$, $\delta$ because it is not clear what is the right quantity

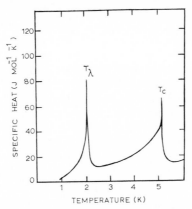

Fig. 7.7. Variation of the molar heat capacity of $^4$He with temperature.

to use as an 'external field' in place of pressure. It also appears that there are no critical scattering peaks associated with the superfluid transition. This suggests that the ordering process that occurs in the superfluid state is intrinsically different from that in a gas–liquid transition. What is observed at the λ transition may be explained, at least qualitatively, by the condensation of statistical-mechanical particles called bosons, rather than in terms of the behaviour of pair correlation functions. Bosons are identical, indistinguishable particles of integral spin. They are not subject to the Pauli exclusion principle, and therefore any number of them can occupy the same energy level. The $^4$He atom is a boson since it contains two neutrons and two protons in its nucleus.

## 7.8. *Thermodynamic inequalities and scaling laws*

It has recently been suggested that the critical exponents of different thermodynamic quantities in the same material are not independent but may be related by various inequalities. The original arguments on which these were based are somewhat dubious, but progress has been made and is continuing to be made in establishing at least some of the relationships on a rigorous basis. Considerations of mechanical and thermodynamic stability require that certain inequalities hold between the indices. Fisher has proved that for a one-component fluid

$$\alpha^- - 2\beta + \gamma^- \geqslant 2$$

and R. B. Griffiths has shown that

$$\alpha^- + \beta(1+\delta) \geqslant 2$$

and

$$\alpha^- + \beta \geqslant \theta$$

where $\theta$ is an index that describes the curvature of the vapour pressure line ($\partial^2 p / \partial T^2$).

It would not be appropriate to consider these in great detail here but they currently provide the basis for some most interesting discussion. For example, consider the first inequality due to Griffiths. Experiments on argon seem to suggest that $\beta \leqslant 0.36$ and $\delta \leqslant 4.4$, in which case $\alpha^- \geqslant 0.05$, which hardly seems compatible with a simple logarithmic divergence for the heat capacity. If the 'best' values of $\beta = 0.345$ and $\delta = 4.2$ are used then $\alpha^- \geqslant 0.20$, which is in even more serious disagreement with experimental observations. If however, $\beta$ and $\delta$ are slightly higher, then the difficulty disappears. Clearly, more refined experimental data are required before these values can be reconciled.

Associated with the search for general relationships that apply to critical exponents are the scaling laws. These are based on rather complicated quantum statistical arguments but they confirm that

110

relations such as those given above should exist near $T_c$, and for example, that $2 - \alpha^- = \gamma^- + 2\beta = \beta(\delta + 1)$. ' Calculations ' for two and three dimensional models show that these laws are obeyed and this fact has encouraged the search for basic fundamental principles as to why this should be the case.

## 7.9. *Future explorations of critical phenomena*

The recent progress in theory and experiment described in this chapter have resulted in a dramatic advance in the understanding of critical phenomena, and most of the fluid investigations have been carried out with the inert gases. Experimentally, some of the technical difficulties such as non-equilibrium and gravitational effects have been recognized and overcome, and values of critical exponents are now being established to a much greater degree of accuracy than was hitherto found possible. In particular, the careful measurement of specific heat has disposed of the possibility once and for all that the phenomenological or van der Waals' fluid theories could be correct in the critical region.

On the theoretical front the progress has been even more striking. It is now quite clear that the interactions that dominate critical phenomena are short-range and that density fluctuations must be taken into account. Thus the van der Waals' type theories are of necessity incorrect, because they assume that the interactions between molecules are long-range, ignore fluctuations in the density and treat $T_c$ as an analytic point. The short-range Ising and lattice-gas models have been solved exactly for two dimensions and some progress has been made with approximate methods towards solving the three-dimensional case. It is not clear whether the Heisenberg and continuum-fluid models offer distinct advantages over the Ising and lattice-gas models in the critical region, although on general grounds one might presume them to be more realistic.

The general progress has been helped also by the recognition that several quite diverse types of phenomena appear to exhibit analogous critical behaviour. One-component fluids, binary solutions, ferromagnets, anti-ferromagnets and binary alloys all display very similar specific heat capacity anomalies. Experimentally determined critical indices, defined in terms of the limiting behaviour of the appropriate experimental parameters, are very similar for all these systems. There is a great deal of interesting work that remains to be done. Theoretically, one must await full solutions to the lattice gas and continuum fluid models. Experimentally, there is a need for careful measurements on almost every type of physical system. Several of the critical exponents need to be fully established so that the scaling laws can be thoroughly tested.

From a statistical mechanical viewpoint, it can be shown that sharp phase transitions can only occur in infinitely large systems. It would be interesting to know whether samples used in experiments were ever sufficiently small for these size effects to be detected. A related question is—what role do boundaries and interfaces play in critical phenomena? All experimental systems in practice are to some extent impure. How does this affect the behaviour? A recent calculation for the three-dimensional lattice gas for example, predicts that the effect of an impurity is nearly independent of its concentration and changes the index $\beta$ from a value of 0·317 for a pure substance to 0·357. Could this explain why experimental values for $\beta$ lie in the range 0·33 to 0·37?

One fact is clear. However dull and unpromising the subject of critical phenomena appeared to be a decade ago, today it forms one of the most exciting and rapidly advancing branches of physics.

# optical and dielectric properties

## 8.1. *Introduction*

THE inert gases are non-polar, because the individual molecule does not possess a permanent dipole moment. In this chapter, the properties of non-polar dielectrics, in which the refractive index or dielectric constant is related to the molecular polarizability (defined below), is reviewed. Because the molecules of the inert gases are monatomic, discussion may be limited to the simple cases in which the polarization is isotropic and due to elastic displacement of the electrons only.

Consider an isolated argon molecule (fig. 8.1). In the absence of an electric field the charge distribution of the electrons about the nucleus

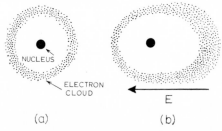

(a)                                (b)

Fig. 8.1.    (*a*) Isolated argon molecule.    (*b*) Symmetry of electron-shell is lost in the presence of an applied field *E*.

is symmetrical. However, when an external field *E* is applied, the electron-cloud is slightly shifted relative to the nucleus and the molecule acquires a temporary induced dipole moment *m* given by

$$m = \alpha E$$

where $\alpha$ is the scalar polarizability. The polarizability is thus a proportionality constant which provides a measure of the distortion produced in a molecule by the electric field.

An argon molecule subject to an external field, but not isolated from other molecules will have an induced dipole moment *m* given by

$$m = \alpha E'$$

where $E'$, the local field, is the field intensity in the neighbourhood of the molecule due to the applied field and also the presence of the other molecules.

113

For gases at low densities, the molecules are sufficiently far apart for the local field intensity to be equated with the applied field. However, when intermolecular distances become comparable with molecular dimensions, an appreciable fraction of the local field intensity is contributed by the electric fields of other molecules. This is true of gases when they are sufficiently dense to depart significantly from the ideal gas law, and of solids and liquids in general.

Provided that the local field may be regarded as being uniform over the small region occupied by the molecule, i.e. the molecules are not too close, the concepts of local field and molecular polarizability are useful and valid. Under conditions of strong interaction, however, these quantities become more questionable, except as average properties of the system. Much effort has gone into calculating the local field in terms of the observed refractive index $n$ and dielectric constant $\epsilon$ of a dielectric. The two are related, since for a non-polar substance $n^2 = \epsilon$, provided that both are measured at the same frequency. Before discussing these methods it is worth reminding ourselves of some basic relationships between electrical quantities. The polarization $P$, or dipole moment per unit volume is defined as

$$P = nm \tag{8.1}$$

where $n$ is the number of molecules per unit volume. The polarization is related to the static dielectric constant $\epsilon$ (i.e. at zero frequency or infinite wavelength) and the electric displacement $D$ by the Maxwell equation

$$D = P + \epsilon_0 E = \epsilon E,$$

which may be written

$$P = (\epsilon - \epsilon_0) E \tag{8.2}$$

## 8.2. *Lorentz theory*

The best known method of calculating the local field intensity in a dense medium was originated by H. A. Lorentz. His derivation has set the pattern for most theoretical treatments of the dielectric constant ever since. For this reason it is worth considering the argument in some detail.

Consider a piece of dielectric subject to an external applied field $E$, the shape being such that the field strength in the material is uniform (fig. 8.2). Select a particular molecule and about it draw a sphere of radius $R$, large in comparison with intermolecular distances but small compared with the macroscopic dimensions of the specimen. The local field intensity $E'$ in the neighbourhood of the molecule may be considered in two parts:

$$E' = E_A' + E_B'$$

where $E_A'$ is the field due to the material outside the sphere, treated as a continuous medium, and $E_B'$ is the field due to the molecules inside the sphere.

114

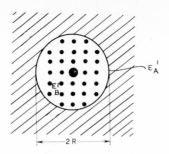

Fig. 8.2.   Lorentz model for a dielectric.

From a macroscopic argument it may be shown that

$$E_A' = E + P/3$$

To compute $E_B'$, some definite distribution of the molecules must be assumed.   The case treated by Lorentz was a cubic lattice of molecules, each electrostatically equivalent to a dipole, and each having the same dipole moment $m$.   He showed that for this model $E_B' = 0$ and therefore

$$E' = E_A' = E + P/3 \tag{8.3}$$

He applied this formula, as an approximation, under somewhat more general conditions.   The resulting expression for the dielectric constant is very simple and has been widely used to describe the properties of gases, liquids and solids.   It is interesting to note that although the limitations on its validity have been largely ignored, Lorentz himself recognized them.

Assuming then that $E_B' = 0$, on the basis that it vanishes for a cubic lattice of dipoles, and is presumably small for any isotropic material, from equations (8.1), (8.2) and (8.3) we obtain

$$\frac{(\epsilon - 1)}{(\epsilon + 2)\,\rho} = \frac{N_A \alpha}{3} \tag{8.4}$$

where $\rho$ is the density and $N_A$ is Avogadro's constant.   Equation (8.4) is known as the Clausius–Mossotti formula and its optical analogue with $\epsilon$ replaced by $n^2$, is the Lorentz–Lorenz formula.   Equation (8.4) predicts that for a given substance the function $(\epsilon - 1)/(\epsilon + 2)\,\rho$ is a constant, independent of density and temperature.

A. Michels and collaborators were the first to have established experimental deviations from equation (8.4) for the inert gases (fig. 8.3). Both dielectric constant and refractive index measurements suggest that $(\epsilon - 1)/(\epsilon + 2)\,\rho$ or $(n^2 - 1)/(n^2 + 2)\,\rho$ increase slowly with increasing density up to roughly critical density and then decrease at higher densities.   More recent measurements on the gas at relatively low pressures and on the liquid confirm this trend.   It is interesting to

115

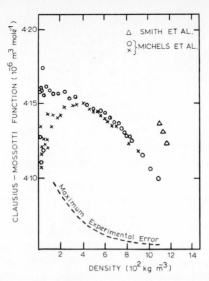

Fig. 8.3. Variation in the Clausius–Mossotti function $(\epsilon-1)/(\epsilon+2)\,\rho$ for argon with change in density of the compressed gas.

speculate why equation (8.4) is not valid. The most obvious flaw concerning a fluid is the assumption of cubic symmetry and in the next section a more acceptable method of calculating the influence of molecular neighbours on the local field is described, based on statistical mechanics.

## 8.3. *Statistical mechanical calculations*

In order to develop a rigorous theory, the molecules must be considered as a complete statistical mechanical system, so that the effect of statistical fluctuations on the induced dipole moment can be properly taken into account. Models which consider only a single molecule and calculate its interactions with neighbours suffer from the defect of the cell model discussed in § 6.3—the effect of interchanges between molecules is not considered. It is still possible, however, to evaluate the mean moment of a single representative molecule; for statistically they are all equivalent.

Suppose that the molecules in a dense system are equivalent to a collection of point dipoles of polarizability $\alpha$, and are spherically symmetric in their other interactions. Assume that the dipoles are in instantaneous equilibrium with the field: that is to say, the instantaneous moment $m_i$ of molecule $i$ is $\alpha E_i'$. If, in the statistical mechanical averaging over possible configurations of the system, the molecules are treated as point centres of force subject to classical laws, then, for this simple model, a rigorous calculation of the dielectric constant is possible.

116

The result may be expressed in the form

$$\frac{(\epsilon-1)}{(\epsilon+2)\,\rho} = \frac{N_A\alpha}{3}\,[1+B\alpha^2+\ldots]$$ (8.5)

The term $B$ has a form similar to that of the second virial coefficient (see § 3.3) and in fact $B$ and other higher terms are sometimes referred to as the second, third etc. dielectric virial coefficients. If only the first term on the right-hand side of equation (8.5) is retained, then the expression reduces to the Clausius–Mossotti formula. The second term $B$ gives a first order correction. To evaluate this correction it is necessary to have values not only of the radial distribution function $\rho(r)$ (or of the equivalent two-molecule distribution $n_2(1, 2)$ which describes the average positions of pairs of molecules), but also $n_3(1, 2, 3)$ which describes the molecules in terms of triplets, i.e. groups of three. For solids with cubic symmetry, such as solid argon, $B=0$ and equation (8.4) should hold. For gases at low pressures, it is possible to express the distribution functions as series, but for liquids this method fails, and as we have seen in Chapter 6, the calculation of even $\rho(r)$ is very difficult. There have, however, been a number of calculations of the dielectric constant of liquid argon using the type of approximations discussed in Chapter 6 and the results of one of these are shown, compared with experimental values for argon in fig. 8.4. As can be seen, although the general course of the experimental curves are reasonably correct, the observed values at higher densities are consistently lower than those predicted theoretically. The reason for this is probably that the polarizability does not remain strictly constant, but may also vary with density.

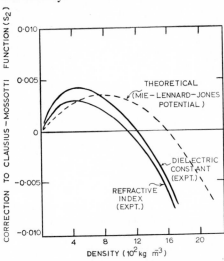

Fig. 8.4.  Comparison of correction to Clausius–Mossotti function ($S_2$) calculated from statistical mechanics with experimentally observed values.

## 8.4. *Variation of polarizability with density*

It would seem reasonable to suppose that at high densities the polarizability α changes significantly from the ' free atom ' value because individual atoms are caged by their neighbours. A calculation of this deviation involves the quantum mechanics of the electronic wavefunctions and is quite complex, involving a ' third-order ' perturbation calculation in order to evaluate even the lowest order correction at moderate densities, and approximate methods at higher densities. The results may be expressed in terms of an effective polarizability at a given density. This is the quantity which, if substituted for α gives the correct mean dipole moments. From this point of view the effect can be described as a variation of the polarizability of a molecule with distance from its neighbours, but from a more fundamental viewpoint, it is questionable whether the polarizability of an individual molecule remains a useful concept when the molecules are tightly coupled. The decrease in polarizability with decreasing intermolecular spacing for argon according to a recent calculation, is shown in fig. 8.5.

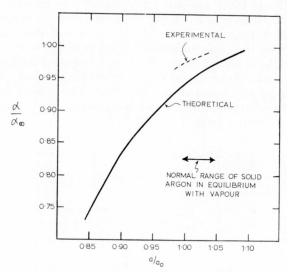

Fig. 8.5. Variation of the polarizability ratio of argon to the free atom value $\alpha/\alpha_\infty$ with the reduced intermolecular spacing $a/a_0$ ($a_0$ refers to the lattice spacing at 0 K).

The effects of statistical fluctuations on the induced dipole moment combined with the change of polarizability with density discussed above are responsible for deviations of the observed behaviour of argon from equation (8.4) (with the possible addition of a small contribution due to quadrupole and higher order interactions). Both effects are present in the liquid and contribute comparably to the deviations. In solid

118

argon, however, only the polarizability effect should be present since it has the cubic symmetry required by the Lorentz model. It might therefore be possible, by comparing accurate experimental results for the liquid and the solid, to distinguish between the two terms.

## 8.5. *Optical measurements in the critical region*

For non-polar substances in general, the lowest frequency at which appreciable absorption of light occurs is usually in the visible or ultra-violet region. In the case of argon, the electronic vibration frequencies are in the far ultra-violet ($\sim 110$ nm) and the dispersion in the visible region is small. A simple Cauchy type relation of the form

$$n = A + B/\lambda^2 + C/\lambda^4$$

where $A$, $B$ and $C$ are constants, and $\lambda$ is the wavelength, is generally adequate to describe the variation of refractive index with frequency, and to extrapolate $n$ to zero frequency, for comparison with dielectric constant values. Since the dielectric constant is measured at relatively low frequencies, a region where the dispersion is almost negligible, only determinations of the highest precision are able to detect any dependence on frequency.

During the discussion of critical phenomena in Chapter 7, a number of critical indices were defined, in order to describe the manner in which fluid properties varied as the critical point was approached. For example, the index $\beta$ is defined in terms of the difference between the liquid and vapour densities along the coexistence curve

$$\rho_l - \rho_v = A(T_c - T)^\beta \qquad (8.6)$$

Experimentally, densities are difficult to measure with great accuracy, particularly in the critical region. If, however, one may assume that the Lorentz–Lorenz function $(n^2 - 1)/(n^2 + 2)\rho$ or its dielectric constant analogue remains constant in the critical region, then measurements of $n$ or $\epsilon$ may be used to determine variations of $\rho$, and hence establish indices such as $\beta$ to a high degree of accuracy. Optical methods based on this principle have been used to study argon and xenon by several investigators, and have the advantage that measurements may be made without perturbing the system either mechanically or thermally. However, very close to $T_c$ the method is suspect since the Lorentz–Lorenz function may be regarded as constant only in a homogeneous medium in which the correlation length associated with density fluctuations is much smaller than the wavelength of the incident radiation. In other words if density fluctuations within the sample became $\sim 500$ nm in size, then equation (8.4) will no longer be valid. Since these fluctuations do exist and in fact give rise to phenomena such as critical opalescence (§ 7.2), values for $\beta$ obtained by this method must be treated with caution.

119

An experiment has recently been carried out in an attempt to determine the magnitude of the possible deviations from equation (8.4), in which the refractive index of a sample of xenon at near critical density was measured by the spectrometric method of minimum deviation. The sample was isolated in a stainless steel cell in which sapphire windows were set at an angle of about 45° to each other in the horizontal plane. The xenon was thus confined in the shape of a prism. The cell was mounted in a cryostat, located at the axis of rotation of an optical spectrometer (fig. 8.6). The refractive index was found from measurements of the prism angle $A$ and the angle of minimum deviation $D$, since $n = [\sin(A+D)/2]/\sin(A/2)$.

Samples of xenon were isolated in the cell at a temperature $\sim 10$ K

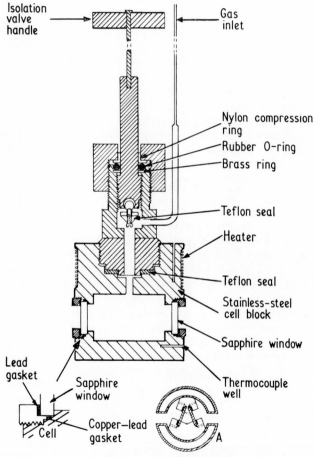

Fig. 8.6. Apparatus used to measure the refractive index of xenon near the critical point. (J. A. Chapman *et al.*, D. Y. Parpia.)

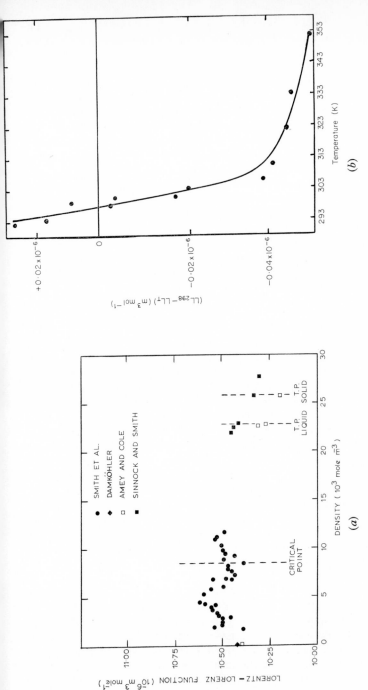

Fig. 8.7. (a) Variation of Lorentz–Lorenz function of xenon with density at 589·3 nm. Values plotted from the results of Chapman et al. are taken from isochores at temperatures which correspond to the co-existence curve. The mean value in the range 1–12 kmol m⁻³ is 10·53 × 10⁻⁶ m³ mol⁻¹. (b) Variation of Lorentz–Lorenz function of xenon with temperature at a density of 8·46 kmol m⁻³ (589·3 nm). The function is normalized to the value (10·39 m³ mol⁻¹) at the isolation temperature (~298 K).

121

above the critical point where the critical effects are not too large. The density was determined by measuring the temperature and pressure, and relating these to previous $(p, V, T)$ data. The angle of minimum deviation was then measured at different temperatures as $T \rightarrow T_c{}^+$. There appeared to be very little variation with change of density, of the values of $(n^2-1)/(n^2+2) \rho$ over quite a wide range of densities (fig. 8.7(a)) and the specific influence of temperature appeared to be very small. At a density very close to $\rho_c$ a small decrease in $(n^2-1)/(n^2+2) \rho$ with decreasing temperature was observed (fig. 8.7(b)), but the change is only just detectable. Periods of several hours were necessary before thermal equilibrium was reached at each temperature and evidence of strong density gradients was seen when $T < 293$ K.

The conclusion that may be drawn from experiments similar to the above is that it is quite legitimate to assume that $(n^2-1)/(n^2+2) \rho$ does not vary by more than $\sim 1\%$ over quite a wide range of thermal states but that it could be misleading to draw too many conclusions based on measurements very close to the critical point. Values for the critical index $\beta$ deduced from optical measurements range from 0·347 for xenon to 0·357 for argon.


## 8.6. Measurements on solid argon

Since the solidified inert gases have the symmetry required by the Lorentz model and the effects due to overlap of the electron shells are probably small, their dielectric behaviour should be described adequately by equation (8.4), provided that $\alpha$ is suitably modified to take account of density. Measurements of the refractive indices of solid argon, krypton and xenon have recently been carried out to test this equation.

The results are interesting because it appears that the density dependence may best be described in terms of the existence of electron-hole pairs, or 'excitons', in the solids. Consider an argon molecule in the crystal lattice (fig. 8.8). Suppose that one of the electrons is displaced from its orbit. There, then exists both a displaced electron and a 'hole' in the orbit where the electron is missing. There is good reason to suppose that the binding-energy between the electron and hole is quantized and that because of this, the electron-hole pairs or excitons, can only have certain allowed spacings or radii associated with them. If the radius is comparable with the molecular diameter, then the exciton is denoted a 'tightly-bound' or 'Frenkel' exciton. If, however, the energy associated with the exciton is somewhat greater, the radius may extent over several atomic spacings, in which case the exciton is a 'Wannier' exciton. Studies of the ultra-violet absorption spectra of the condensed inert gases suggests that both types might exist in the solids (fig. 8.9), because absorption peaks are observed that correspond to the predicted energies of the excitons.

How are excitons related to optical and dielectric properties? Absorp-

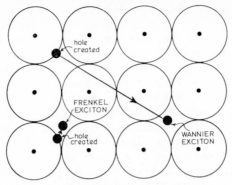

Fig. 8.8. Electron moves away from atom creating an electron 'hole'. If the distance is ~ the atomic radius $r$, the electron-hole pair is regarded as tightly bound (Frenkel exciton). If the distance $>r$, Wannier excitons are formed.

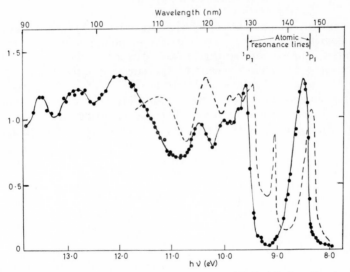

Fig. 8.9. Absorption spectrum for solid xenon (G. Baldini). Continuous line $-19$ K. Dashed line $-53$ K.

tion doublets (fig. 8.9) are found in the solids close to the atomic resonance doublets observed in the low density gases. These have energies and radii that are intermediate in size (i.e. slightly larger than atomic radius) and may be considered to be associated with either the first excitons in Wannier series, or else to tightly-bound excitons of the Frenkel type. Since calculations of the polarizability and experimental data indicate that the number of electrons that contribute to the di-electric properties of argon is about $8 \cdot 7$ and the ground-state configuration

123

of argon is $KL3s^23p^6$, this suggests that only the outer electrons contribute significantly (see § 1.4), and hence a tight-binding model, based
on lowest energy level transitions, might be adequate to describe the
density dependence of the dielectric properties to a reasonable degree of
accuracy.

This approach has been adopted by S. Doniach, R. Huggins and other
investigators. They considered the atoms in solid argon to act as
localized electron oscillators, coupled with each other only by nearest-
neighbour forces. The dielectric properties are assumed to result
mainly from the lowest level ultra-violet band ($^{3,1}P_1 \rightarrow {}^1S_0$ transition),
which can be represented by a single line of the type associated with a
Frenkel exciton. Doniach and Huggins supposed that the energy (or
frequency) of the exciton depended only on the density, and deduced
that the Clausius–Mossotti functions should be given by

$$3\frac{(\epsilon-1)}{(\epsilon+2)}\frac{1}{\rho}=\frac{\omega_p{}^2}{(\omega_0{}^2+V_0{}'''(\rho)-\omega^2)}+X_1=X_0+X_1 \qquad (8.7)$$

In spite of its apparent complexity, equation (8.7) merely describes
the interactions between molecules represented by simple harmonic
oscillators coupled with springs, a pair of which is shown in fig. 8.10.
Each atom is considered to consist of a 'shell' of outer electrons and a
'core' of inner electrons and the nucleus. The total interaction
therefore consists of the sum of a shell–shell term, two shell–core terms
and a core–core term as represented by springs in fig. 8.10. In equation (8.7), $\omega_p{}^2$ is the shell–shell force and is a dipole–dipole interaction

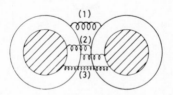

Fig. 8.10. Shell model for spherical molecules showing the interactions
between the 'shell' of outer electrons and 'core' of inner electrons
and nucleus. (1) Shell–shell (dipole–dipole) force; (2) Shell–core
force; and (3) Core–core (weak) force.

of the van der Waals type discussed in § 2.3. (Sometimes $\omega_p$ is called
the plasma frequency). $\omega_0$ is the natural frequency of the non-interacting atomic oscillators ($\omega_0 \gg \omega$), i.e. the shell frequency of a free
atom. $V_0{}'''(\rho)$ corresponds to the shift in $\omega_0{}^2$ observed with increasing
density, and due to the shell–core interactions. $\omega$ is the frequency at
which the dielectric constant $\epsilon$ is measured. The core–core forces are
assumed to be negligible compared with the shell–shell and shell–core
interactions and are omitted. However, an extra term $X_1$, assumed to

be frequency independent, was introduced to take account of the core polarizability and possible contributions to the exchange integrals (electron cloud overlap) from higher atomic states. Comparing equation (8.7) with equation (8.4), if $\chi_1$ is ignored. $\omega_p{}^2$ is equivalent to $4\pi N_A \alpha$ and $(\omega_0{}^2 - \omega^2)$, modified slightly by $V_0{}'''(\rho)$, describes the dispersion.

The validity of this model has recently been tested by A. C. Sinnock and the author by measuring the refractive indices of solid argon, krypton and xenon as a function of frequency over a wide range of temperature, and hence density. The results were fitted to equation (8.7) using a computer to extract the optimum values of $\omega_p{}^2$ and $\chi_1$ by the method of least squares. The natural frequencies $\omega_0$ were set equal to the lowest energy transition in the gas (in spectroscopic terms this is the mean of the spin-orbit split doublet $^{1,3}P \rightarrow {}^1S_0$). $V_0{}'''(\rho)$ was assumed to vary with the density according to a simple exponential function. The results for solid argon are shown as continuous lines

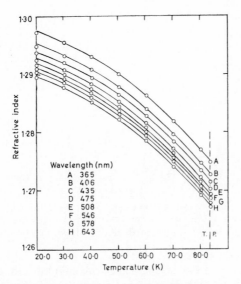

Fig. 8.11. Comparison between the experimental refractive index of solid argon (○) and theoretical curves fitted by equation (8.7) (continuous line).

in fig. 8.11, where they are seen to represent the experimental values extremely well.

Of course, one should not be too impressed with the agreement between theory and experiment observed in fig. 8.11, because the theoretical parameters were derived directly from the experimental data. A better test of the model is to use the values of the parameters to determine the exciton frequency $\omega_{ex}$, which of course may be measured

125

directly by an absorption experiment. This is related to $\omega_0$, $V_0{}'''(\rho)$, $\omega_p$ and $\chi_1$ by

$$\omega_{\text{ex}}{}^2 = \omega_0{}^2 + V_0{}'''(\rho) - \frac{\omega_p{}^2}{9}\left[\frac{(2\chi_1+3)}{(3-\chi_1)}+2\right] \qquad (8.8)$$

Using equation (8.8), together with values for the parameters extracted from the refractive index data for solid argon, one finds that a shift in frequency ($\omega_{\text{ex}} - \omega_0$) is predicted that varies with density as shown in fig. 8.12. Unfortunately, the observed shifts are somewhat

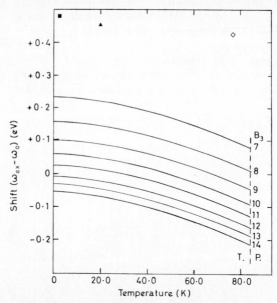

Fig. 8.12. Variation of exciton frequency shift for solid argon with temperature. The continuous lines are derived from equation (8.8) for various plausible values of $V_0{}'''(\rho)$. ■, ▲, ◇, experimental observations.

larger. However, it may be that one is being unrealistic in applying data from a region of low absorption (weak coupling) to predict properties in a region of high absorption (strong coupling). A recent very careful quantum mechanical calculation has confirmed that about 95% of the total polarizability of an argon atom is due to the $3p^6$ electrons, with most of the density dependence due to variations in this contribution, as implied by the tight-binding model.

## 8.7. *Other optical experiments on the solidified inert gases*

Apart from the refractive index measurements described above, several other significant optical experiments on the solidified inert gases have recently been reported. M. Creuzburg and K. Teegarden have detected luminescence in solid krypton. Large samples (15 mm × 5 mm) were grown in a plastic tube from the liquid. They were then irradiated with 25 kV, 17 mA X-rays from a copper source and the emission spectrum analysed. At 80 K two prominent bands were found at about 4·2 and 5·5 eV (fig. 8.13). As the temperature was lowered to 20 K the 5·5 eV band increased while the 4·2 eV band gradually diminished and disappeared. During prolonged irradiation at this temperature two new emission bands appeared—a sharp line at 4·2 eV and a broader band at 4·1 eV. After the X-rays had been shut off, weak emission was detected at 5·5 eV when the crystal temperature was raised. Analysis of samples grown from krypton that contained impurities resulted in a number of sharp spectral lines that were interpreted as being due to the vibrational energy levels of the impurities. The impurities also had the effect of reducing the intensity of the bands shown in fig. 8.13. Since the nearest electronic absorption band is

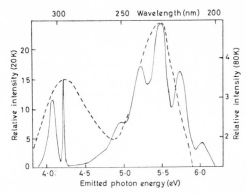

Fig. 8.13. Luminescence in solid krypton at (a) (continuous line) 20 K, (b) (dashed line) 80 K after ∼5 ks irradiation by X-rays.

∼10 eV, the luminescence bands thus appear to be due to some type of colour centre formed in the krypton lattice by the X-ray irradiation. Whether or not these centres are similar to those found in alkali halides remains to be seen. The electronic structure is somewhat similar, but the simple non-impurity centres in the alkali halides are strongly influenced by the ionic interaction, which of course is absent in the solidified inert gases. Various resonance investigations, Faraday rotation and other experiments are in progress to establish the nature of these intrinsic centres. It has also been suggested that laser action might be produced by excitation with an electron beam.

Since the solidified inert gases are transparent to radiation ranging from the ultra-violet to the infra-red, they provide a convenient tool for studying molecular spectra. For example, by trapping molecules in an inert gas lattice, the effect of an environment on the absorption spectrum and hence on the energy levels may be examined. Diatomic carbon frozen in a solid xenon lattice is experimentally equivalent to a quantum mechanical harmonic oscillator trapped in a small box. The effect of the environment of xenon atoms on the spectra may be estimated, either theoretically by calculating the interaction, or experimentally by varying the density (changing the temperature), and noting the differences in the spectra produced by the changing intermolecular distances. Changing from solid xenon to argon or krypton is equivalent to changing the size of the box.

## 8.8 *Magneto-optical properties*

The inert gas molecules are not optically active in the sense that they cause rotation of plane polarized light in the absence of a magnetic or electric field. However, small electro-optical and magneto-optical effects are observed and the study of these can provide useful additional information about molecular polarizabilities and in the condensed state, inter-molecular forces.

The only property that has been systematically studied is the Faraday effect, i.e. the rotation of the plane of polarization of plane polarized light when it passes through a substance in the direction of an applied magnetic field. The degree of rotation is described by the Verdet constant $V$, which is the rotation per unit path length per unit field strength for a substance and is defined by

$$V = 2.98 \times 10^{-4} E \frac{\mathrm{d}n}{\mathrm{d}E} \text{ radian}$$

where $E$ is the energy of the incident radiation.

The dependence of $V$ on density can be calculated using a model very similar to the Lorentz local field model discussed in § 8.2. The model leads to a quantity $\Omega$ which should be independent of state and hence is analogous to the Lorentz–Lorenz function:

$$\Omega = \frac{9n}{(n^2 + 2)^2} \frac{V}{\rho}$$

where $n$ is the refractive index and $\rho$ is the density. $V/\rho$ is sometimes referred to as the specific rotation. The Verdet constant, $\Omega$ and the specific rotation of gaseous, liquid and solid argon are given in Table 8.1. As can be seen, the effect is extremely small, even for solid argon, and accurate measurements are therefore extremely difficult.

A careful investigation of the Verdet constant of the condensed inert gases has recently been carried out by H. V. Mølgaard, using a cryostat with the sample placed between the poles of a powerful electromagnet, (fig. 8.14). Monochromatic light from a spectral lamp is made parallel by means of a lens and the beam is then carefully collimated. The light passes through a polarizing Nicol prism and is made plane polarized.

Table 8.1.  Verdet constants of gas, liquid and solid argon, at $\lambda = 546 \cdot 1$ nm.

| State | Verdet constant, $V^*$ (minute G$^{-1}$ m$^{-1}$) | Density, $\rho$ kg m$^{-3}$ | Refractive index | $\dfrac{9n}{(n^2+2)^2}$ | $V/\rho$ (minute G$^{-1}$ m$^2$ kg$^{-1}$) | $\dfrac{V}{\rho}\dfrac{9n}{(n^2+2)^2}$ (minute G$^{-1}$ m$^2$ kg$^{-1}$) |
|---|---|---|---|---|---|---|
| Gas at 273 K and 101·3 kNm$^{-2}$ pressure | $10 \cdot 25 \times 10^{-4}$ | $1 \cdot 78$ | $1 \cdot 000$ | 1 | $5 \cdot 76 \times 10^{-6}$ | $5 \cdot 76 \times 10^{-3}$ |
| Liquid 86·1 K | $[8 \cdot 72 \pm 0 \cdot 2] \times 10^{-1}$ | $1 \cdot 402 \times 10^3$ | $1 \cdot 230$ | $0 \cdot 8971$ | $6 \cdot 25 \times 10^{-6}$ | $5 \cdot 60 \times 10^{-3}$ |
| Solid 80·5 K | $[9 \cdot 61 \pm 0 \cdot 2] \times 10^{-1}$ | $1 \cdot 630 \times 10^3$ | $1 \cdot 270$ | $0 \cdot 8758$ | $5 \cdot 87 \times 10^{-6}$ | $5 \cdot 14 \times 10^{-3}$ |

* The SI unit for $V$ is rad T$^{-1}$ m$^{-1}$.  The conversion factor to bring the tabulated values to rad T$^{-1}$ m$^1$ is approximately $3 \cdot 4 \times 10^7$

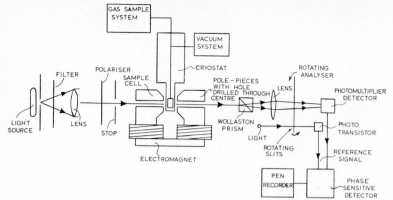

Fig. 8.14.   Apparatus used to measure Faraday rotation in the inert gases.

It then passes through holes drilled in the electromagnet pole pieces and through the sample between them.   Before reaching the analyser, the beam is split into two plane polarized components by a Wollaston prism.   The analyser is a second Nicol prism, kept rotating at about 20 revolutions per second.   The light signal is detected by a photo-multiplier tube and the output fed to an electronic phase-sensitive detector.   As the analyser rotates it passes alternately the two com-ponents from the Wollaston prism.   A switching device, synchronized to the analyser, allows the phase sensitive detector to receive and com-pare the magnitudes of the two signals.

The Wollaston prism is first set with the magnetic field at zero so that the two components are exactly equal and the phase sensitive detector gives a small reading.   When the magnetic field is applied, the small rotation of the plane of polarization causes the two components to differ by an amount indicated on the detector.   The angle by which the Wollaston prism has to be rotated in order to restore the null value, recorded from an accurate circular scale in which it is mounted, is a direct measure of the Faraday rotation.

These types of measurement are only in their infancy.   Future investigations of both magneto-optical and electro-optical properties will no doubt prove to be of immense value in furthering understanding of the effects of local field on molecular properties.   Examination of solid samples in spectral regions where luminescence has been noted, and in which defects have been created or impurities injected, should also help to establish the types of intrinsic centres possible in the con-densed inert gases.

inert gas compounds

9.1. *Introduction*

UNTIL about 1962, the inert gases appeared to be truly inert, and apart from highly unstable species such as $He_2^+$, HeH and HgXe, the only known chemical compounds were clathrates, in which inert gas atoms are trapped in chambers formed by other molecules. This lack of chemical activity is of course due to their electronic configuration. All the inert gas atoms have valence shells that are closed and quite stable (see Chapter 1). The only forces that operate between pairs of inert gas molecules are the weak van der Waals dispersion forces, proportional to the polarizability and inversely proportional to the ionization potential of the atoms. They depend on the size and diffuseness of the electron clouds surrounding the nucleus and increase with increasing atomic number.

The recent discovery that the inert gases can take part in genuine chemical reactions therefore came as a considerable surprise, although it is interesting to note that as early as 1930, L. Pauling had predicted the formation of exothermic inert gas fluorides. During the past few years chemical compounds of krypton, xenon and radon have been prepared. As would be expected, the chemical activity of the molecules increases with decreasing ionization potential and also with the energy required to place the atom in an unpaired electron state—the promotion energy (Table 9.1). For this reason, most of the work to date has been carried out on xenon. The chemical activity of radon is presum-

|  | Configuration of outer shell | First ionization potential (eV) | Promotion energy (eV) |
|---|---|---|---|
| He | $1s^2$ | 24·6 | — |
| Ne | $2s^2 2p^6$ | 21·6 | 16·6 |
| Ar | $3s^2 3p^6$ | 15·8 | 11·5 |
| Kr | $4s^2 4p^6$ | 14·0 | 9·9 |
| Xe | $5s^2 5p^6$ | 12·1 | 8·3 |
| Rn | $6s^2 6p^6$ | 10·8 | 6·8 |

Table 9.1. Electron configuration, ionization potential and promotion energy required for the $ns^2 np^6 \rightarrow ns^2 np^5 (n+1) s$ transition. According to present knowledge, the threshold of actual chemical activity is only reached at krypton.

ably greater but the α-radioactivity and short half-life make experimental work both hazardous and technically difficult.

## 9.2. *Xenon compounds*

Xenon reacts directly with one element only, namely fluorine. This reaction is possible because of the relatively low ionization potential of xenon, and the high electron affinity of fluorine. Other compounds of xenon must be obtained indirectly via the xenon fluorides. The stable compounds $XeF_2$, $XeF_4$ and $XeF_6$ are prepared by mixing xenon and fluorine in the appropriate proportions and heating the mixture under correct conditions. $XeF_4$ for example, which is the easiest compound to prepare, is formed when a 1 : 5 mixture of xenon and fluorine is heated in a nickel can at 670 K under about 0·6 MNm$^{-2}$ pressure for several hours. (In principle, of course, the ratio of xenon to fluorine should be 1 : 4, but in practice, the excess fluorine increases the rate at which chemical equilibrium is reached.) All the fluorides are white crystalline solids, with very polar (directional) covalent bonds. It is interesting to note that they are isoelectronic with known iodine compounds, i.e. the molecules have the same number of valence electrons and therefore have similar molecular orbitals associated with them. For example, $XeF_4$ is isoelectronic with $IF_4^-$ and both are square planar molecules ($sp^3d^2$ hybrid Xe).

The bonding of the xenon fluorides may be described by a conventional technique used in modern chemistry—molecular orbital theory. There is no need, as some originally supposed, to invoke a new type of bonding to describe the compounds. The bonding is most easily discussed for the simpler molecules $XeF_2$, although similar arguments apply to $XeF_4$ and $XeF_6$. The bonds are due to the overlapping of σ-type atomic orbitals (fig. 9.1). (An orbital is a representation of the quantum-mechanical electron cloud distribution: a σ orbital is an atomic orbital that is symmetric about the axis.) The overlap is between the $2p\sigma$ orbitals of the two fluorine atoms, $F_A$ and $F_B$, and the $5p\sigma$ orbital of xenon. The most plausible arrangement turns out to be a linear system in which the positive lobes of the $2p\sigma$ orbitals are directed towards the xenon atoms and the outer part of the $5p\sigma$ orbital of xenon overlaps positively with the left-hand fluorine $2p\sigma$ orbital. It will then overlap negatively with the right-hand fluorine $2p\sigma$ orbital. This arrangement has the greatest binding-energy and predicts a charge-distribution for $XeF_2$ of roughly $F^{-1/2} - Xe^{+1} - F^{-1/2}$. (In $XeF_4$ and $XeF_6$, the positive charge associated with the Xe atom increases.) The detailed theory shows why an even number of F ligands is favoured (i.e. $XeF_2$, $XeF_4$, $XeF_6$) and also underlines the importance of the ionization potential of the central atom, together with the need for a small and electronegative ligand. The quantitative predictions are in substantial agreement with the results of nuclear magnetic resonance measurements on the xenon fluorides.

132

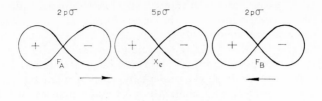

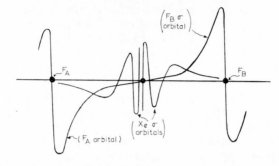

Fig. 9.1. (a) Atomic orbitals for $XeF_2$. (b) Radial parts of the $2p\sigma$ atomic orbitals of fluorine and the $5p\sigma$ atomic orbital of xenon at an internuclear distance corresponding to the $XeF_2$ molecule.

Xenon tetrafluoride dissolves in water to give $XeO_3$:

$$3XeF_4 + 6H_2O \rightarrow 2XeO_3 + Xe + 12HF$$

and on evaporation, white hygroscopic crystals of xenon trioxide $XeO_3$ are left. These are explosive. However, $XeO_3$ is also very strong and exceptionally clean as an oxidizing agent, since the by-product of oxidation is xenon gas itself. It may be used either directly, or in the perxenate form $Na_4XeO_6 \cdot 8H_2O$, obtained by dissolving $XeO_3$ in a strong solution of NaOH.

### 9.3. Inert gas clathrates

Prior to the successful preparation of the xenon fluorides, the only inert gas compounds known were the clathrate crystals. In these compounds the inert gas atoms are trapped in chambers formed by other molecules interacting with each other by the formation of hydrogen bonds. The 'guest' atoms or molecules in a clathrate are held in position by van der Waals forces in a crystalline cage consisting of the 'host' molecules. Although the bonding is weak, a clathrate is a true chemical compound, exhibiting some stoichiometry, i.e. the number of guest molecules that may be held in a unit cell is limited. A simple clathrate may be designated by a formula $nH.mG$, where $H$ and $G$ refer to the host and guest components respectively: $n$ is the number of host molecules per unit cell (cage), and $m$ is the maximum number of guest molecules that may be held in a single cage.

133

The inert gases form clathrates with hydroquinone, phenol and several other compounds but the most simple are the hydrates of argon, krypton and xenon. These are single phase crystals in which $n = 46$ and $m = 8$ in the clathrate formula given above. Thus there is a maximum of one guest atom per 5·75 molecules of water. The exact ratio is difficult to establish experimentally, since it is hard to determine exactly when the hydrate contains the maximum quantity of inert gas. However, experimental values support that $n/m \approx 6$.

In the inert gas hydrates, the water molecules are linked together by hydrogen bonds, leaving roughly spherical voids which are occupied by the gas atoms. X-ray diffraction shows that in the cubic unit of structure, with edge 1·2 nm, there are 46 water molecules arranged in a framework such that each water molecule is surrounded tetragonally by four others, with which it forms hydrogen bonds with lengths roughly the same as in ordinary ice (0·276 nm). Each unit cell contains eight chambers. Two of these are defined by 20 molecules at the corners of a nearly regular pentagonal dodecahedron, and the other six are bounded by 24 water molecules at the corners of a tetrakaidecahedron with two hexagonal and 12 pentagonal faces (fig. 9.2). Each chamber may be occupied by one molecule.

The stability of the hydrates is partially due to the van der Waals interaction between the trapped molecules and the water molecules in the framework and partially due to the energy of the hydrogen bonds. The stability of the unfilled framework might be expected to be identical with that of ice, but because the hydrate is rather more open than ordinary ice, the added stabilization of the water molecules due to van

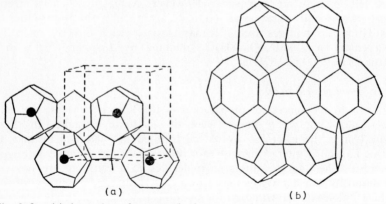

(a)  (b)

Fig. 9.2. (a) A portion of a xenon hydrate crystal showing the structure with some of the xenon atoms (●) in position. There are 46 water molecules per unit cube, of which two sets of 20 are at the corners of pentagonal dodecahedra. The other six hold the dodecahedra together. (b) Another view of a xenon hydrate crystal. Each dodecahedron (centre) is surrounded by tetrakaidecahedra. Six tetrakaidecahedra and two dodecahedra form a unit cube.

der Waals interaction is less than that of ice by about $0.7 \text{ kJ mol}^{-1}$. The hydrates may be formed very simply by dissolving an inert gas in water under pressure and then lowering the temperature. The dissociation pressure at 273 K and the decomposition temperature of the crystals under atmospheric pressure ($\sim 101 \text{ kNm}^{-2}$) for each hydrate is given in Table 9.2.

| Ig | Decomposition temperature at 101 kN m$^{-2}$ pressure (K) | Dissociation pressure at 273 K (MN m$^{-2}$) | Heat of formation (kJ mol$^{-1}$) | Crystal lattice constant (nm) |
|---|---|---|---|---|
| Ar | 230·4 | 10·6 | — | — |
| Kr | 245·4 | 1·47 | 58·2 | — |
| Xe | 269·8 | 0·15 | 69·9 | 1·197 |

Table 9·2.   Properties of the inert gas hydrates (Ig).5.75H$_2$O.   (No hydrates of He or Ne have yet been prepared.)

The interaction between the trapped inert gas atoms and the surrounding water molecules is easily estimated from the London equation for the electronic dispersion forces. The energy of interaction $W$ between two molecules $A$ and $B$, with polarizabilities $\alpha_A$ and $\alpha_B$ (see § 8.1), and excitation energies $E_A$ and $E_B$, is given by

$$W = -\frac{3}{2} \frac{\alpha_A \alpha_B}{r^6} \frac{E_A \cdot E_B}{(E_A + E_B)}$$

where $r$ is the distance between their centres. In the 8Xe.46H$_2$O crystal, the two xenon molecules that are in the pentagonal dodecahedral chambers are surrounded by 20 water molecules at a distance of 0·385 nm, and the six xenon molecules in the tetrakaidecahedral chambers are 0·403 nm from 12 of their water neighbours and 0·55 nm from the other 12. The average energy of a xenon atom can thus be estimated to be about 43 kJ mol$^{-1}$, 5 kJ of which arises from interactions with second nearest neighbours.

About 34 kJ mol$^{-1}$ is required to form Xe.5.75H$_2$O from gaseous xenon and ice, thus correcting for the difference in energy between the hydrate and ice structures, the total energy of formation of 8Xe.46H$_2$O is therefore $43 + 35 - 0.7 = 77.3$ kJ mol$^{-1}$. Some measured properties of the inert gas hydrates are given in Table 9.2. Note that the observed heat of formation is in rough agreement with the value calculated above. It is also interesting to note that the heats of adsorption of inert gases on activated charcoal (e.g. xenon 36·4 kJ mol$^{-1}$) are of the same order of magnitude as the van der Waals binding of the inert gas atoms within the hydrate.

135

# CHAPTER 10
## applications of the inert gases


10.1. *Introduction*

Throughout most of this book, the emphasis has been placed on the role of the inert gases as model substances. However, there are many other areas in physics, particularly near the boundaries, where their special properties make them particularly valuable for research. In astrophysics, for example analysis of the inert gas content of minerals and meteorites helps to date the origin of the universe. Current studies of inert gas diffusion in metals may solve a vitally important problem encountered in nuclear reactors. The anaesthetic properties of xenon have led to a ' physical ' theory of anaesthesia. Inert gas lasers provide physicists with a powerful probe with which to investigate the properties of liquids. These are a few examples chosen to illustrate the present-day use of the inert gases in quite diverse branches of physics.

The above applications all depend to some extent on the inert properties of the gases. For example, radioactive dating of minerals would become impossible if the stable gas isotopes reacted with neighbouring atoms. The anaesthesia caused by xenon in the higher animals and man would become a chemical-bonding rather than a physical problem. If the inert gases created by thermal neutrons in a reactor were chemically active they would pose a corrosion threat as well as a cause of structural damage. Even producing an inert gas laser would be much harder if the gas reacted chemically with impurities within the laser tube.

It is only fair to point out that the quantities of inert gases involved in the investigations described here represent only a minute fraction of the total annual industrial and laboratory production. Over a billion cubic feet of argon ($28 \, Mm^3$ at NTP) are extracted throughout the world each year. About $68\%$ of this amount is used as a shielding gas in the arc welding of metals, a further $28\%$ is used to provide inert atmospheres for metallurgical processes, and $2\%$ is used in electric light bulbs and fluorescent lamps. The rarer gases, krypton and xenon (atmospheric contents—1 and $0 \cdot 09$ parts by $10^6$ by volume) are produced in much smaller quantities—the author's laboratory accounts for a substantial proportion of the annual British output of xenon. At the other end of the scale, some of the less common isotopes, produced only as by-products of nuclear reactions in machines, are available only in the minutest amounts.

## 10.2. Radioactive dating of the universe

The gases argon and helium are important in methods used to determine the origin of minerals and meteorites, and hence to assign ages to parts of the universe. These methods are based on the positions of stable argon and helium isotopes in radioactive decay series, and assume that, in a statistical sense, radioactive disintegration has taken place at a constant rate since the universe was first formed. Uranium and thorium both emit $^4$He ($\alpha$-particles) as they decay, and radioactive $^{40}$K disintegrates into the stable isotopes $^{40}$Ar and $^{40}$Ca.

The uranium–helium method consists of determining the amounts of uranium and helium present in the mineral to be dated (fig. 10.1), and then calculating the age from the ratio, assuming a value for the decay rate. An obvious source of error arises if some of the helium diffuses out of the sample during the long time period ($\sim 10^9$ years), and for this reason only mineral samples that are effectively non-porous may be used. There are two checks on the consistency of the results that may be made. Firstly, there are other stable products in addition to helium produced in the decay of uranium—isotopes of lead, for example, and these may be analysed and used to confirm an age calculation. Secondly, a laboratory determination of the activation energy for diffusion of helium through a sample of the mineral will establish the extent to which the material is non-porous. A small but significant correction has to be applied to the results to account for the $^3$He that has been produced from the $^4$He by nuclear transformation due to cosmic radiation.

The more recent potassium–argon dating method is similar to the above but has a number of important advantages. Foremost is the lower diffusion rate of argon relative to helium, because of the larger molecular diameter. Also important is the fact that most rocks contain some potassium, whereas only a limited number contain uranium or thorium. One problem that initially created difficulty is the need for an accurate knowledge of the 'branching ratio' for the number of $^{40}$K atoms that decay to $^{40}$Ar relative to the number that decay to $^{40}$Ca. Historically this ratio proved to be hard to determine experimentally. However, it is now well established at a value of about 0·11.

A problem encountered with both helium and argon dating is that an unusually high concentration of these gases is found in certain minerals. Terrestrial beryl, cordierite and tourmaline crystallized from magma about $2\cdot7 \times 10^9$ years ago. The proportion of $^4$He and $^{40}$Ar that could be expected to have been produced in these minerals from radioactive decay is in some cases less than 1 per cent of the total found by analysis—up to 100 cm$^3$ of $^4$He and 32 cm$^3$ of $^{40}$Ar per kg. The most likely explanation is that the helium and argon were already present in these minerals at the time that they were formed. They all have in common an atomic structure that is based on a six-membered

**URANIUM SERIES**

URANIUM–238
$\alpha \downarrow$ ($1 \cdot 4 \times 10^{17}$ s)
THORIUM–234
$\beta \downarrow$ ($2 \cdot 1 \times 10^{6}$ s)
PROTACTINIUM–234
$\beta \downarrow$ ($2 \cdot 4 \times 10^{4}$ s)
URANIUM–234
$\alpha \downarrow$ ($7 \cdot 6 \times 10^{12}$ s)
THORIUM–230
$\alpha \downarrow$ ($2 \cdot 5 \times 10^{12}$ s)
RADIUM–226
$\alpha \downarrow$ ($5 \cdot 0 \times 10^{10}$ s)
RADON–222
$\alpha \downarrow$ ($3 \cdot 3 \times 10^{5}$ s)
POLONIUM–218
$\alpha \downarrow$ ($3$ s)
LEAD–214
$\beta \downarrow$ ($1 \cdot 6 \times 10^{3}$ s)
BISMUTH–214
$\beta \downarrow$ ($1 \cdot 2 \times 10^{3}$ s)
POLONIUM–214
$\alpha \downarrow$ ($1 \cdot 6 \times 10^{-4}$ s)
LEAD–210
$\beta \downarrow$ ($6 \cdot 2 \times 10^{8}$ s)
BISMUTH–210
$\beta \downarrow$ ($4 \cdot 3 \times 10^{5}$ s)
POLONIUM–210
$\alpha \downarrow$ ($1 \cdot 2 \times 10^{7}$ s)
LEAD–206
(Stable)

**ACTINIUM SERIES**

URANIUM–235
$\alpha \downarrow$ ($2 \cdot 3 \times 10^{16}$ s)
THORIUM–231
$\beta \downarrow$ ($9 \cdot 4 \times 10^{4}$ s)
PROTACTINIUM–231
$\alpha \downarrow$ ($1 \cdot 1 \times 10^{12}$ s)
ACTINIUM–227
$\beta \downarrow$ ($7 \cdot 0 \times 10^{8}$ s)
THORIUM–227
$\alpha \downarrow$ ($1 \cdot 6 \times 10^{5}$ s)
RADIUM–223
$\alpha \downarrow$ ($1 \cdot 1 \times 10^{6}$ s)
RADON–219
$\alpha \downarrow$ ($3 \cdot 9$ s)
POLONIUM–215
$\alpha \downarrow$ ($1 \cdot 8 \times 10^{-3}$ s)
LEAD–211
$\beta \downarrow$ ($2 \cdot 2 \times 10^{2}$ s)
BISMUTH–211
$\beta \downarrow$ ($1 \cdot 3 \times 10$ s)
POLONIUM–211
$\alpha \downarrow$ ($0 \cdot 52$ S)
LEAD–207
(Stable)

**THORIUM SERIES**

THORIUM–232
$\alpha \downarrow$ ($4 \cdot 4 \times 10^{17}$ s)
RADIUM–228
$\beta \downarrow$ ($2 \cdot 8 \times 10^{8}$ s)
ACTINIUM–228
$\beta \downarrow$ ($2 \cdot 2 \times 10^{4}$ s)
THORIUM–228
$\alpha \downarrow$ ($6 \cdot 1 \times 10^{7}$ s)
RADIUM–224
$\alpha \downarrow$ ($3 \cdot 1 \times 10^{5}$ s)
RADON–220
$\alpha \downarrow$ ($5 \cdot 1 \times 10$ s)
POLONIUM–216
$\alpha \downarrow$ ($0 \cdot 16$ s)
LEAD–212
$\beta \downarrow$ ($3 \cdot 8 \times 10^{4}$ s)
BISMUTH–212
$\qquad \alpha \rightarrow$ ($3 \cdot 6 \times 10^{3}$ s)   THALLIUM–208
$\beta \downarrow \qquad$ POLONIUM–212 $\qquad\qquad \beta \downarrow$ ($1 \cdot 8 \times 10$)
$\qquad \alpha \downarrow$ ($3 \times 10^{-7}$ s)   LEAD–208
(Stable)

Fig. 10.1. Principal radioisotopes in the uranium, actinium and thorium series, together with decay times (1 year $= 3 \cdot 15 \times 10^{7}$ s).

138

tetrahedral ring. Since helium and argon were being produced in the atmosphere at the time that the earth was formed, by outgassing of the earth's lower crust, these gases may have been occluded within the channels defined by the six-membered rings. As the mantle cooled, the outgassing presumably decreased. The partial pressures of the helium and argon in the region of the magma were reduced and less gas was occluded. This proposal accounts for the observation that the helium and argon content of beryl and cordierite is found to increase with the age of the mineral.

Let us examine the potassium–argon method in greater detail. The radioactive isotope $^{40}K$ decays to $^{40}Ar$ and $^{40}Ca$ by a branched decay scheme (fig. 10.2) in which about 89% of the disintegrating nuclei end in

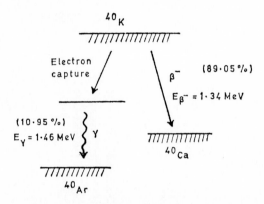

Fig. 10.2. The $^{40}K$ isotope decays to $^{40}Ca$ by $\beta$-emission and to $^{40}Ar$ by K-capture to an excited state, followed by $\gamma$ emission.

$^{40}Ca$ and 11% end in $^{40}Ar$. The half life is $1 \cdot 26 \times 10^9$ years, which implies that about $10^3$ atoms disintegrate per kg every three seconds in a typical sample of igneous rock. In $10^6$ years this is equivalent to $10^{16}$ atoms. Hence, since a sensitive mass spectrometer is capable of measuring samples of $\sim 10^{13}$ atoms with moderate precision, rock specimens as small as $\sim 10^{-3}$ kg may be examined by this method. At first sight it may appear that the dual decay offers the possibility of two determinations of decay rate and hence two estimates of age. However, in practice, $^{40}Ca$ is too abundant a geological material, and the detection of the small radiogenic increment on the normally large background is technically difficult and results in a large possible error.

The $^{40}K$–$^{40}Ar$ half-life of $1 \cdot 26 \times 10^9$ years is ideal for dating a great range of geological time and is particularly suited for dating younger minerals. In addition to terrestrial sampling, the method has been used extensively to determine the age of meteorites. The apparatus required consists of three parts—a gas extraction system and separate detection systems for the argon and potassium. A typical extraction system used to examine meteorites is shown in fig. 10.3.

In this apparatus, a sample of predetermined mass from the meteorite is loaded into a crucible which is then carefully evacuated at a temperature of about 473 K. This is sufficient to remove gases occluded in the walls of the container but should not alter the argon content of the specimen. A background of $^{38}$Ar isotope is then admitted to the container to act as a carrier gas. The sample is completely vaporized by a powerful electrical heater to a temperature of about 1800–2100 K. The gases emitted are cleaned by putting them in contact first with cold titanium wire and then titanium sponge. The argon is then adsorbed on charcoal at the temperature of liquid nitrogen.

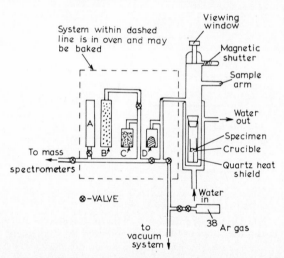

Fig. 10.3. Gas extraction and purification system used in argon analysis. *A*, calibration gas. *B*, charcoal. *C*, titanium wire. *D*, titanium sponge.

At this stage, the absolute quantity of argon present and the isotope ratio $^{40}$Ar/$^{38}$Ar may be determined using two mass spectrometers. These are conveniently Nier-type devices, similar to the instrument described in § 10.3 for use as a detector in connection with diffusion measurements. Both are highly sensitive devices, equipped with Faraday collectors and electron multipliers, in addition to pipettes which contain inert gas mixtures for use in calibrating the ion beam intensity.

The potassium content may be determined chemically, but this is a time-consuming and difficult procedure. Flame photometry now provides a more convenient and powerful analytical tool. In this method a solution containing potassium is placed in a hot flame. The characteristic radiation, produced when the flame-excited atoms return

140

to ground state, is filtered, detected by a photocell, and the current produced amplified. Using a carefully calibrated sample the potassium content may be established to about $\pm 0.5\%$ by this technique, this being the major source of error in the age determination.

The potassium–argon method of dating is of particular value in dating certain types of rock, including geologically ' young ' samples which are difficult to date by other methods. For example, analysis of the potassium–argon content of samples taken from Hawaii have shown that the order of cessation of volcanism occurred along the island chain from north-west to south-east. The detailed figures show that the minimum velocity of convection currents in the earth's mantle is $\sim 0.1$ m per year and also lend credence to estimates of age based on geomorphological arguments. Using this method whole geological regions have been mapped out on a time-scale with an accuracy hitherto thought to be impossible (fig. 10.4).

One other application of great interest is the dating of meteorites, which until very recently, provided the scientist with the only source of extraterrestrial material for direct laboratory analysis. Meteorites have only two general categories—stony and iron, with a range of types intermediate between these two. Typical chemical compositions of meteorites are compared with the contents of the earth's crust in Table 10.1. Stony meteorites are roughly similar in appearance to heavy igneous rocks and iron meteorites, which have an 80–90% iron content, are heavier, and appear slightly metallic (fig. 10.5). The ages of stony meteorites are found to range from about $4.8 \times 10^9$ years to less than $10^9$ years, which may be compared with $\sim 4.5 \times 10^9$ years for the oldest rocks found on the earth. The reason for this large range is not clear; but the presence of cosmic-ray-produced nuclei recorded in meteorites, together with their size and shape, suggests that all of these bodies underwent at least one collision that broke them from larger, pre-existing masses. The data for iron meteorites are more controversial but indicate that they were formed $\sim 4.8 \times 10^9$ years ago. If these ages are confirmed by subsequent measurements, then they will support the suggestion that meteorites were formed as a result of collisions between planets roughly the same size and composition as the earth, as a result of which iron meteorites emerged from the iron-rich cores, and stony meteorites were produced from the outer crusts. A laboratory simulation of an asteroid-planet collision, helpful in this kind of investigation, is shown in fig. 10.6.

There are of course other methods for determining the age of geological specimens by the use of radioactive dating. For example, the use of strontium 87–rubidium 87 has now become a viable technique. But historically, uranium–helium played an important role and today argon–potassium still remains a most valuable tool for probing the past. It must be emphasized that in these experiments, the samples available for analysis are often extremely small. It is only by using extreme

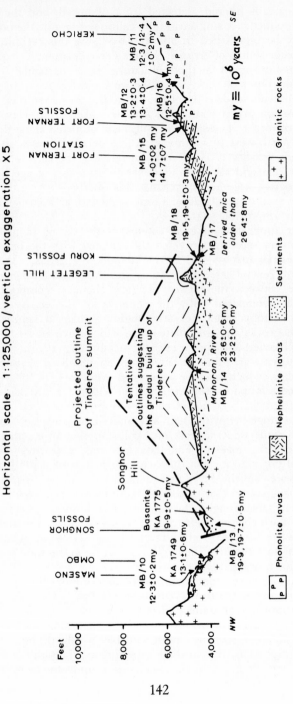

Fig. 10.4. Cross section through the Songhor, Koru and Fort Ternan (Kenya) fossiliferous localities, showing regions dated by the argon–potassium method. (Bishop *et al.*, 1969.)

142

| Element | Fe | Ni | Co | P | S | C | Cu | Cr | $O_2$ | Si | Mg | Al | Ca | Mn | K | Ti | Na |
|---|---|---|---|---|---|---|---|---|---|---|---|---|---|---|---|---|---|
| Earth | 4·7 | 0·02 | — | 0·12 | — | — | — | 0·03 | 49·4 | 25·8 | 1·9 | 7·5 | 3·4 | 0·08 | 2·4 | 2·4 | 2·6 |
| Iron | 90·8 | 8·5 | 0·59 | 0·17 | 0·04 | 0·03 | 0·02 | 0·01 | — | — | — | — | — | — | — | — | — |
| Stony | 25·6 | 1·4 | 0·14 | 0·19 | — | — | — | 0·27 | 36·3 | 18·0 | 14·2 | 1·5 | 1·3 | 0·18 | 0·13 | 0·10 | 0·06 |

Table 10.1.   The percentage composition of the earth's crust compared with that of typical iron and stony meteorites.

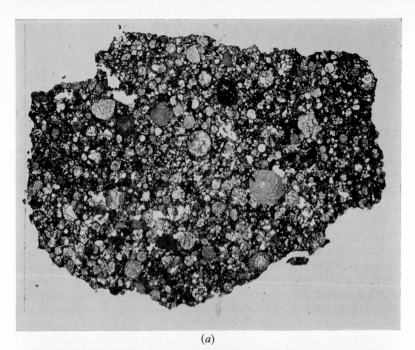

(a)

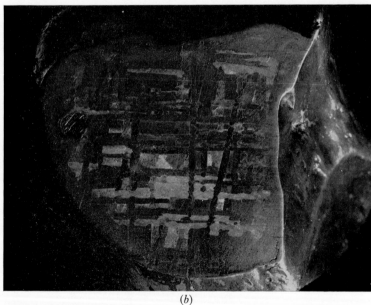

(b)

Fig. 10.5. (a) Section of typical stony meteorite displaying well developed chrondules (Prairie Dog Creek). (b) Etched face of the Rowton iron meteorite showing alloy impurity patterns. (Courtesy of the trustees of the British Museum.)

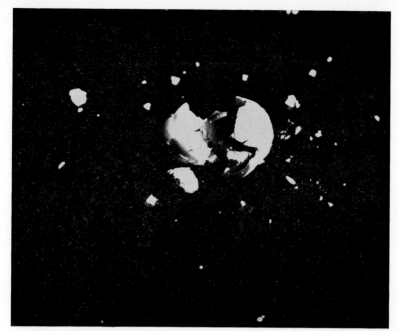

Fig. 10.6.   Typical example of the result of a model asteroid colliding with a
    target of effectively infinite mass at subsonic speed.   The use of layered
    and thermally treated models, with crust, mantle and core, provides a
    dramatic test of the postulated theories of the origin of meteorites.
    (Photograph by J. W. McClanahan from Wasserburg and Burnett 1969.)

precautions to avoid contamination and by pushing the analytical techniques to their utmost limits of precision and accuracy that reliable and
consistent results can be obtained.

## 10.3.   *Inert gas bubbles in nuclear reactor materials*

The inert gases play an important role in the radiation damage
produced in materials by nuclear bombardment, because the reactions
often include an inert gas as a byproduct.   Examples of the more
common reactions resulting from collisions between atoms and thermal
neutrons are given in Table 10.2.   The inert gases are also sometimes
ejected as high-speed particles which may cause damage while in flight,
and may come to rest inside a solid, introducing impurity atoms into the
material.

The solubility of gases in normal metals and other solids is generally
very small indeed.   However, it has been observed that the materials
used in the construction of nuclear reactors, when subjected to radiation
damage at elevated temperatures, often exhibit marked changes in

145

| Reaction | Cross-section (unit: 1 barn = $10^{-28}$ m$^2$) | Inert gas product |
|---|---|---|
| $^6$Li$(n, \alpha)^3$H | 950 | He |
| $^{10}$B$(n, \alpha)^7$Li | 3990 | He |
| $^{25}$Mg$(n, \alpha)^{22}$Ne | 0·27 | He and Ne |
| $^{235}$U$(n,$ fission$)$ | 14 | Kr |
| $^{235}$U$(n,$ fission$)$ | 46 | Xe |

Table 10.2.  Some nuclear reactions produced by thermal neutrons that result in the production of inert gas atoms.

physical dimensions.  At room temperature an increase of 1–2 per cent is found, which is roughly the amount expected due to the presence of gaseous byproducts from nuclear reactions in interstitial positions. As the temperature rises, however, the changes become more considerable.  In metallic uranium, for example, the 1–2 per cent increases to $\sim 100$ per cent at 773 K, and is observed as gross swelling and distortion of the material.  Such an effect on fissile material, coupled with the possibility of similar changes taking place in vessel walls, obviously has alarming consequences from the point of view of reactor design. Strenuous efforts are currently being invested in research programmes designed to determine the causes of swelling, the main mechanism of which appears to be the formation of gas bubbles within the solid.

More information about the mechanism of gas-bubble formation in reactor fuel elements and structural materials is being sought in extensive research studies, the basis of which is the use of an accelerator to inject helium atoms into metal specimens by bombardment with $\alpha$ particles.  Uniform gas concentrations ranging from $10^{-6}$ per cent to about 1 per cent can be introduced into layers of metal $\sim 10^{-4}$ m thick by this method. Various techniques, including measurements of lattice parameter (spacing between atoms) and electrical resistivity, are then used to obtain relevant information.  To illustrate the results obtained to date, a typical series of electron microscope pictures of irradiated copper are shown in fig. 10.7.  At room temperature little effect on the material is observed, even after a long period of annealing.  At 1070 K however, bubbles soon begin to form.  At first these are confined to regions close to grain boundaries or near the sample surface, but in due course they grow in size and become more evenly distributed throughout the irradiated section.  Careful analysis of the size and motion of gas atoms and bubbles, suggests that helium atoms alone are not able to form bubbles, but require the presence of vacancies.  These are produced either from grain-boundaries or from free surfaces by thermal activation.

Support of this hypothesis comes from a series of lattice parameter measurements on copper, samples of which were first irradiated and

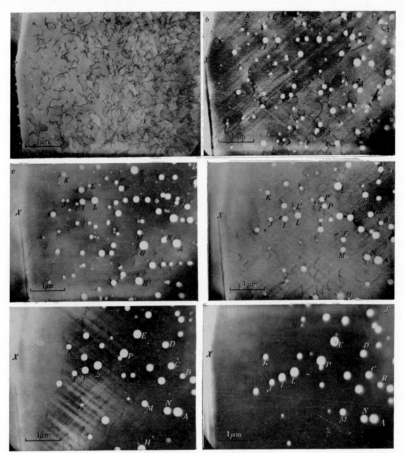

Fig. 10.7. Electron micrographs of Cu containing $0.1\%$ $^4$He showing effect of annealing at $\sim 1070$ K. (a) Bubbles $< 10$ nm in diameter form on dislocation network produced by the irradiation. (b) Bubbles grow in size and are redistributed. (c) Further growth and coalescence takes place. (d) Further migration and coalescence. Some bubbles (e.g. $G$) have been lost to the surface. (e) Further annealing. Note that $P$ has a small satellite bubble. (f) More bubbles have disappeared. The satellite has rotated around $P$. (Barnes and Mazey 1963.)

then annealed at temperatures in the range 573–1073 K for several hours (fig. 10.8). It was found that irradiation initially caused a small increase in lattice dimensions. This amount is consistent with the presence of helium atoms in interstitial positions, i.e. between atoms on lattice sites, which distort the lattice. When annealing commences, the initial increase gradually disappears, presumably as a result of each helium atom combining with one or more vacancy, until the lattice

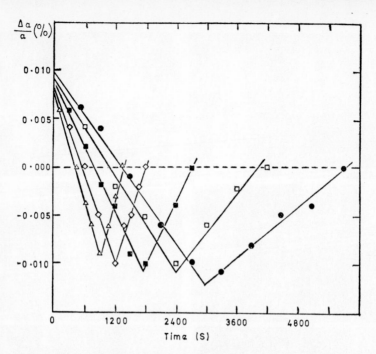

Fig. 10.8. The percentage variation of the lattice parameter of Cu as a function of annealing time. ●, 823 K; □, 848 K; ■, 873 K; ◇, 898 K; △, 923 K. (Russell and Hastings, 1965.)

eventually becomes smaller than its original size. Further annealing results in these (helium + vacancies) complexes migrating through the crystal and coalescing to form bubbles. It is the growth of these bubbles that eventually leads to the gross distortion and swelling that is sometimes observed in a lattice, and which can pose a serious hazard in a reactor.

Although electron-microscopy is invaluable in studying the growth and migration of bubbles once they have reached a certain size ($\sim 2 \ \mu m$), the resolution ($\sim 2$ nm) is not good enough to examine the early stages leading up to formation. However, information concerning the initial kinetics of stable bubble growth can be obtained by measurements of gas diffusion. All the existing experimental evidence suggests that inert gas atoms diffuse through metals in exactly the same way as do metallic impurity atoms. It is therefore possible to apply all the usual theoretical and semi-empirical rules for inter-metallic diffusion to determine the diffusion mechanism, the type of site occupied and the effective size and charge state of an inert gas atom in a metallic lattice. Investigations with the lighter inert gases confirm that the gas atoms are retained in neutral closed-shell form and diffuse *via* the vacancy

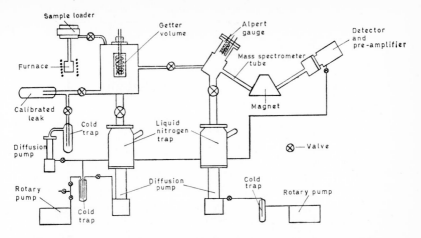

Fig. 10.9. Apparatus used to measure diffusion of helium in silver.
(Courtesy of H. R. Glyde.)

mechanism. Diffusion studies can decide for example, whether a particular inert gas is trapped in a given metal and can trace the migration kinetics up to the point at which all the gas is trapped. Measurements can also determine the distance that atoms migrate before becoming trapped.

A typical experimental arrangement that is being used for diffusion studies of $^4$He in silver at the University of Sussex, is shown in fig. 10.9. Small samples of metal foil are irradiated on the Harwell variable energy cyclotron so as to produce atomic concentrations of helium ranging from $10^{-2}$ to $10^{-6}$ per cent. Each sample is then annealed in a stainless-steel furnace at a carefully controlled temperature. The quantity of inert gas evolved is monitored as a function of time using an ultra-high vacuum mass spectrometer. This is a Nier type single-sector magnetic focusing machine which uses a uniform magnetic field to analyse mono-energetic ions of differing specific charge. It is constructed entirely of non-magnetic stainless steel and is regularly baked at $\sim 620$ K to reduce background levels.

The degree of irradiation of samples is chosen so that the fraction of gas atoms arriving at the surface without being caught by a trapping site is sufficient for accurate measurement. Minute concentrations are used so as to minimize radiation damage in the crystal. Some typical results for silver which demonstrate how the irradiation (concentration) affects the time taken for atoms to become trapped in bubbles are shown in fig. 10.10.

The mechanism of trapping and the initial stages of bubble formation are complex and only partially understood at present. Most investigations have been carried out with helium and very little work has yet been performed with the heavier inert gases. Because the properties of

F                                    149

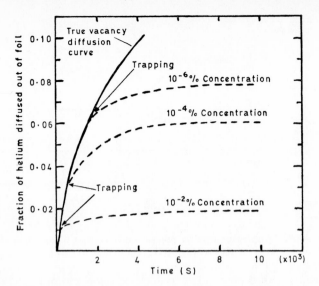

Fig. 10.10. Amount of helium diffusing out of a silver foil as a function of time. Note that trapping occurs earlier at higher concentrations. (Courtesy of D. H. Garside.)

each sample depend critically on its metallurgical history, the most useful investigations are those in which different techniques are applied to sections taken from a single sample. For example, diffusion measurements and electron microscope studies yield complementary information, and provide a possible bridge between single and multiple atom processes.

There are many questions concerning bubble formation as yet unanswered at present and it is now recognized that study of the creation and properties of inert gas clusters in solids constitutes a research area of the utmost technological importance.

## 10.4. Molecular theories of anaesthesia

Research interest in the biology of the inert gases has on the whole been motivated by practical considerations. Helium has been used medically in physiological applications because, relative to nitrogen, it has a lower density and a lower solubility in water and fatty substance (lipid) found in several parts of the body. Thus helium–oxygen mixtures are used to treat patients with obstructions in the larynx and trachea, and are supplied as safe atmospheres to underwater divers. In the first case, the work of breathing is considerably reduced because of the smaller density of the mixture and in the second, decompression following surfacing can be carried out much more rapidly than when pressurized air is used because of the smaller quantity of gas dissolved

in the blood.  (Dissolved nitrogen causes ' drunkenness of the deep '.)
There are many other applications, involving both stable and radioactive
isotopes, but in this section attention will be confined to one specific
physical problem—how a chemically inert gas such as xenon can cause
narcosis and anaesthesia in mammals and other higher animals.

During the past two decades considerable progress has been made in
understanding biological phenomena in terms of the structure of
molecules and their interactions with each other.  Attempts have been
made to describe mechanisms such as consciousness, memory, narcosis
(dullness—in extreme cases, unconsciousness), sedation and similar
psychobiological phenomena using the techniques of molecular physics.
It is generally supposed that consciousness and ephemeral memory
involve electric oscillations in the brain, whereas permanent memory
is associated with a material pattern, in part inherited (instinct) and in
part transferred from the ephemeral memory.  The nature of the
electrical oscillations and their interactions are not known in detail,
but their existence is clearly shown in measurements of the brain
activity, where the recorded patterns (electroencephalograms) are seen
to depend both on the state of consciousness and the mental activity of
the subject under investigation.

The ephemeral memory is clearly established as electrical in nature
and does not last for longer than a few minutes, unless conscious attention is directed to it.  Experiments show that when an electric shock of
sufficient intensity to cause unconsciousness is administered to a subject,
it often causes a complete loss of memory of events experienced during
the 10–15 minutes preceding the shock.  The detailed processes that
occur at a molecular level are obviously extremely complicated but for
the present purposes it is sufficient to use arguments based on a quite
simple model, first proposed by Linus Pauling in 1961.

The electrical oscillations of consciousness and ephemeral memory
may be discussed in terms of the exciting mechanism and the supporting
structure.  The supporting structure is the brain, with its network of
neuroglial cells, neurones and synaptic interneural connections, that
determine the detailed nature of the oscillations.  The energy of the
oscillations depends both on the exciting mechanism and the impedance
of the neural network.  A reduction in brain activity such as occurs in
sleep or in general anaesthesia may be due to either a decrease in the
excitation energy, or an increase in the impedance of the neural network,
or a combination of both factors.  Whereas it is probable that some
sedatives (e.g. barbiturates) and some stimulants (e.g. caffeine) may
operate by altering the level of activity of the exciting mechanisms, it
appears likely that general anaesthetics of the non-hydrogen-bonding
type are effective because they increase the impedance of the brain.  The
mechanism for this, according to Pauling, is the formation of minute
hydrate microcrystals of the clathrate type.

This suggestion is immediately attractive because of the large number of substances known to cause general anaesthesia, among them argon (under pressure) and xenon. The chemical properties of these substances are such that it is unlikely that narcosis is produced by chemical reactions in which ordinary chemical bonds are formed or broken. It is known that the formation and rupture of hydrogen bonds play an important role in many physiological processes, but the inert gases would not be expected to form even weak hydrogen bonds.

The only property shared by these 'physical' anaesthetics is their ability to form clathrate crystals (see § 9.3). In the hydrates, the 'guest' molecules are trapped in chambers formed by water molecules, interacting with each other by the formation of hydrogen bonds. The bonding of the 'guest' molecules in the crystalline cage is weak and depends only on the van der Waals interactions between the molecules.

The observed narcotic effects obtained with xenon are shown in Table 10.3. Clearly the simple mechanism of hydrate formation

| System | Pressure kN m$^{-2}$ | Effect |
|---|---|---|
| Man | 80 | Total anaesthesia |
| Mouse | 60–80 | Partial narcosis |
| Dog | 80 | Partial narcosis |
| Cockroach | 314 | Partial narcosis |
| Drosophila (fruit fly) | 80 | Decreased O$_2$ consumption |

Table 10.3.  Effects of xenon on various biological systems.
(101·3 kN m$^{-2}$ = 1 atmosphere pressure).

described above is inadequate to describe the observations, since at room temperature and at 80 kN m$^{-2}$ pressure ($\sim 0.8$ atmospheric pressure), one would not expect the 8Xe.46H$_2$O compound to be stable (Table 9.2). It is therefore reasonable to suppose that some other stabilizing influence is also operative, perhaps connected with the side chains of protein molecules and solutes in the encephalonic fluid. These might work in conjunction with the xenon to form a more complex and stable hydrate. Molecules of the anaesthetic agent will then occupy some of the chambers of the hydrate crystal, while others are occupied by groups of molecules from those normally present in the brain. Such a combination could produce microcrystals that are sufficiently stable to persist at temperatures 10–15 K higher than would be possible if no anaesthetic agent were present. (Narcosis, i.e. decrease in activity and possible unconsciousness, is produced in the human brain by cooling it (hypothermia) to about 300 K, i.e. about 10 K below normal blood temperature.)

There is one further interesting piece of evidence that lends support to the hydrate crystal hypothesis. The energy of interaction between

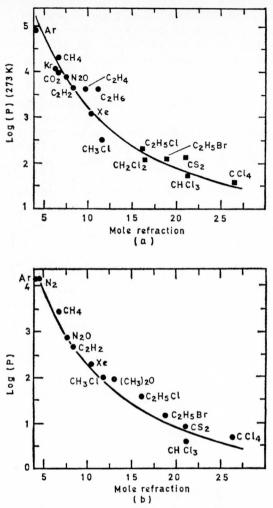

Fig. 10.11. (*a*) Variation of the logarithms of the partial pressures of anaesthetic agents (in equilibrium with their hydrate crystals) with their mole refractions. ●, Ig.5·75 H₂O crystals as discussed in the text, ■, larger molecules can only occupy tetrokaidecahedra, hence these hydrates correspond to Ig.7·66 H₂O. (Ig≡the guest molecule.) (*b*) Logarithm of the partial pressure required for the anaesthesia of mice plotted as a function of the mole refraction of the anaesthetizing agent.

the water framework and the trapped molecules is directly proportional to the mole refraction $R = (\epsilon - 1)/(\epsilon + 2)\rho$ of the trapped molecules (see §§ 8.2 and 9.3). One would expect that the interaction energy for different hydrates would vary such that the greater its size, the smaller the pressure required for the hydrate to be stable. This is observed experimentally (fig. 10.11(a)). Also found experimentally is that the partial pressure required to anaesthetize mice varies with the mole refraction of the anaesthetizing agent in much the same way (fig. 10.11(b)). The correlation between pressures measured in the two experiments is very striking (fig. 10.12).

Of course, the microcrystalline theory of anaesthesia may eventually be proved wrong. Certainly at this time, however, the evidence that the anaesthetizing action observed with non-hydrogen-bonding agents depends on interaction with the molecules in the brain via van der Waals forces is very convincing. Experiments with the inert gases are currently under way that may help to establish these processes more clearly.

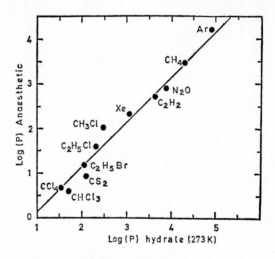

Fig. 10.12. Correlation between the logarithms of the anaesthetizing partial pressures of non-hydrogen bonding anaesthetic agents and the logarithms of the equilibrium partial pressures of their hydrate crystals.

Anaesthesia is just one aspect of the physiological effects of inert gases on living tissues, and some of the other effects ought to be mentioned briefly. Under appropriate conditions the inert gases produce various degrees of narcosis, decreased response to stimuli, alteration of metabolism and changed rate of development in many organisms. Except in the case of metabolism, the effects of the different gases increase with increasing molecular weight. Some of the properties of the inert gases are of great practical importance for human beings, for example, the use of helium mixtures as an atmosphere in aviation and in diving operations has already been mentioned. Others have not yet reached the stage of exploitation, for example, the use of xenon as an X-ray opaque medium in certain diagnostic procedures, or as a radiation protection agent in the radio-therapy of cancer. It is quite clear, however, that the inert gases are playing an increasingly important role in biology and medicine.

## 10.5. *Inert gas lasers*

Light amplification by the stimulated emission of radiation (laser) is a process that has developed during the past decade into a technique of immense practical importance. The helium–neon laser, and more recently the argon–ion laser, are of fundamental interest in themselves and provide valuable tools for investigating other systems. Although in reality the laser process is both subtle and complicated, the somewhat over-simplified approach adopted here should suffice to establish the main principles.

There are several advantages that a laser possesses compared with a conventional light source. Firstly, the great intensity of the output allows Rayleigh scattering and other weak processes to be investigated. Secondly, the light is very monochromatic. Thirdly, the radiation is *temporally coherent* in the sense that the phase and amplitude is predictable along each wavetrain, and *spatially coherent* in the sense that phase relationships between the light at different positions across the beam are fixed.

Consider a system of atoms of a single element, each atom being capable of occupying one of two energy states, the ground state or an excited state. Excitation of an atom to a higher energy state followed by relaxation to the ground state is accompanied by energy losses (i.e. light emission) via the emission of independent, randomly phased wave packets of finite length. The resultant intensity is a product of the number of excited atoms per unit time which emit radiation ($n$) and some mean amplitude squared ($\bar{a}^2$). If, however, a means can be found whereby all the atoms could be forced into emitting their waves in phase, then the resultant intensity is increased to ($n^2\bar{a}^2$). This in simple terms is the principle of the laser.

For a laser system to function, conditions must be created in which the atoms are stimulated to emit at a frequency $v$ in response to an oscillating electromagnetic field of the same frequency. In practice, the system is placed between two mirrors so that standing waves are set up and it becomes in effect a cavity resonator. The electrical analogy (which must not be pressed too far!) is a tuned oscillator circuit with a feedback system and a power supply (fig. 10.13($a$)). The portion of emitted radiation that is reflected and then stimulates further emission between energy levels then plays a similar role to that of electrical feedback.

In terms of the two-level energy model (fig. 10.13($b$)), three processes are possible: (a) atoms in level 1 may absorb energy $h\nu_{12}$ and become excited to level 2, (b) excited atoms may spontaneously return to 1 by emission of $h\nu_{12}$ and (c) atoms in level 2 may be stimulated by the radiation field to return to level 1, in which case the stimulated emission is

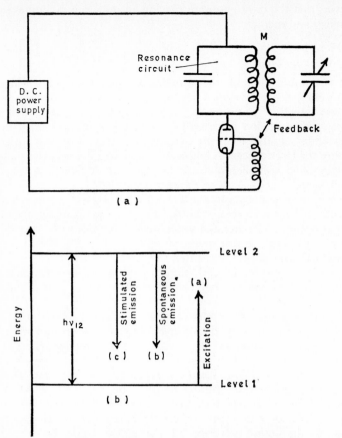

Fig. 10.13.   (a) Electrical oscillator equivalent of a laser system.   (b) Two-
level energy system for an atom.

(Courtesy of L. Allen and D. G. C. Jones)

coherent with the stimulating emission.   Process (c) allows a standing
wave to build up between the mirrors, equivalent to the resonance at a
specific frequency obtained in the tuned circuit.   Since the mirrors do
not reflect 100% of the radiation, power must be supplied to the
system continuously to replace energy losses and to re-excite the atoms to
their upper energy level.   A two-level system in thermal equilibrium
has a population of electrons in level 2 that is less than that of level 1,
because the number $n$ is governed by the Boltzmann equation:

$$n \propto \exp\left(-E/kT\right)$$

where $E$ is the energy of a level.   One would normally find that

$$(n_2/n_1) = \exp\left(h\nu_{12}/kT\right) \approx 10^{-10}$$

156

but for stimulated emission to take place a *population inversion* must be created so that $n_2 > n_1$.

The first gas laser was successfully demonstrated in 1961 when A. Javan and co-workers succeeded in producing oscillations at five frequencies close to each other in a helium–neon mixture. The mode of operation of this laser may be understood by reference to the energy level diagrams shown in fig. 10.14. The long-lived but metastable

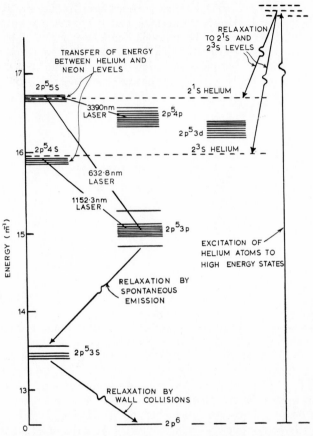

Fig. 10.14. Energy level diagram of neon showing the principle of the helium–neon gas laser. (Energy = $h\nu \propto \mathrm{m}^{-1}$)

energy state $2^3S$ of helium is very close energetically to the neon excited state which corresponds to the $2p^54s$ configuration. Because of this proximity, inelastic collisions which result in a transfer of excitation energy from the metastable state of helium to the excited state of neon are quite probable. Such processes are known as collisions of the second kind.

157

The spread of the energy levels in the $2p^54s$ configuration is small ($\sim kT$), and these levels become heavily populated with respect to the $2p^53p$ configuration, which in turn decays quickly to the metastable $2p^53s$ level. Javan obtained oscillations at five frequencies, the strongest output power ($\sim 15$ mW) of which corresponded to a wavelength of 1152·3 nm. (This is the $4s^1P_1{}^0 - 3p^3P_2$ transition in the spectroscopic $L$–$S$ coupling notation.)

Since 1961 a very large number of other laser frequencies have been obtained for the helium–neon system, and it remains by far the most common type of laser. The red 632·8 nm line (fig. 10.14) is easily obtained and the construction of a low power He–Ne laser has now become a relatively simple task. The basic elements of such a laser are shown in fig. 10.15. A typical power requirement is $\sim 200$ watts of

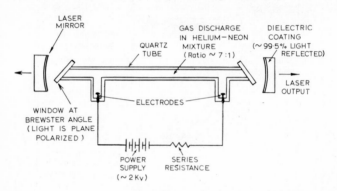

Fig. 10.15. Experimental arrangement of a simple helium–neon gas laser.

excitation and a continuous wave (c.w.) output ranging from 0·5 to 50 mW can be produced. The major advantages of a gas laser over a pulsed solid-state laser, apart from its continuous operation, is that the output is more nearly monochromatic, more stable, and more directional. It is thus useful for a wide range of applications, including the testing of optical devices, length and distance determinations and many specific measurements, particularly of the ' scattering ' type.

Lasers have now been developed for many gases and gas mixtures, with the result that outputs are available at hundreds of different wavelengths. An important device that has recently been developed is the singly ionized argon (Ar II) laser. The result of passing an extremely large d.c. or r.f. current through a low pressure argon is to ionize the argon atoms. The ions have sufficient excitation to produce laser oscillation of considerable intensity at several frequencies. These correspond to $p \to s$ transitions among the lowest lying excited electronic levels (fig. 10.16), and by ' tuning ' the laser, continuous outputs of several watts can be obtained at several wavelengths in the blue-green

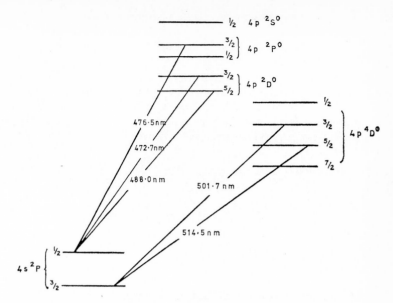

Fig. 10.16. Energy levels and some c.w. transitions for the Ar II laser.

region. Only singly ionized levels have been found to work continuously and the exciting mechanism appears to be a two-step electron impact one. The advantage of having a high power output in the blue visible region is that radiation detection is more convenient. From the viewpoint of scattering investigations, because the scattering intensity generally varies inversely with some power of the wavelength, a shorter wavelength increases the scattered intensity significantly.

Many types of experiment are now made possible by the advent of a powerful single-frequency c.w. light source as represented by the argon ion laser, and to illustrate this by an important application, this section is concluded by a summary of the types of information that may be obtained by a series of scattering measurements on a simple liquid, for example, liquid argon. Light is scattered from fluctuations in refractive index, which in turn result from fluctuations in density. According to the Ornstein–Zernicke theory, the fraction, $R$, of light scattered per unit solid angle is given by

$$R = \left[ \left( \rho \, \frac{\partial n}{\partial \rho} \right)^2 \frac{\pi^2 L}{\lambda_0^4} \, kT \right] \left[ \frac{1}{1 + K^2 a^2} \right] k_T$$

where $L$ is the length of the scattered region, $k$ is Boltzmann's constant, $T$ is the absolute temperature, $\rho$ is the density, $k_T$ is the isothermal compressibility and $a$ is the correlation length—a characteristic length

159

which describes the fluctuations.   The scattering vector

$$K = \frac{4\pi n}{\lambda_0} \sin \theta/2$$

refers to light of wavelength $\lambda_0$ scattered at an angle $\theta$, and $n$ is the refractive index.   If the density and the refractive index of the liquid are known, then the compressibility may be determined by extrapolating the scattered intensity, measured as a function of angle, to zero angle. This procedure is particularly valuable for investigations into the critical region (see § 7.2).

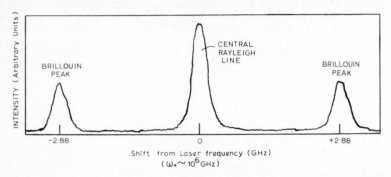

Fig. 10.17.   Frequency spectrum of light scattered from liquid argon showing shifted Brillouin lines.   The shift of 2·88 GHz which is observed corresponds to a phonon velocity of 850 m s⁻¹. (P. A. Fleury and J. P. Boon, 1969.)

In addition to the scattered intensity observed at the unmodified laser frequency, an examination of the frequency spectrum (fig. 10.17) shows that there are subsidiary peaks—Brillouin lines, which appear at slightly different frequencies.   These represent inelastic scattering processes in which radiation gains or loses energy in collisions with the fluid molecules.   The process is rather similar to the Doppler shift. Measurements of the small frequency shift ( ~ 3 GHz) of the Brillouin peaks using a high resolution Fabry–Pérot interferometer allows the adiabatic sound velocity $v$ and the high-frequency longitudinal modulus of elasticity $M_\infty$ to be investigated ($M_\infty = \rho v^2$).   The frequency examined is considerably higher than that available in an ultrasonics (high frequency sound) experiment: hence by comparing the results with low frequency data, the possibility of velocity dispersion effects arising from structural relaxation in the liquid may be studied.

If a mechanism should exist in the liquid that damps the thermal waves (phonons), the Brillouin lines are broadened, and the ultrasonic absorption coefficient, $\alpha$, may be determined from the line width.   This absorption is caused in general by shear and volume viscosities and by the thermal conductivity of the liquid. (Shear viscosity is the normal viscosity: bulk or volume viscosity is associated with interchange of kinetic and potential energy within the fluid, i.e. the fluid expands or contracts during flow.) Since the thermal conductivity should have negligible influence in the case of liquid argon, the Brillouin line width is related to a linear combination of the two viscosities. Hence for regions in which the shear viscosity is known, the volume viscosity may be estimated. (At temperatures approaching the critical temperature $T_c$, the shift becomes small and the lines are broadened by a rapid increase in sound absorption, hence the method fails because of the loss of resolution.)

In addition to the 'internal' properties described above, surface effects may be investigated with a laser. The viscous damping of thermal excitations on the interface of a two-phase system may be examined by determining the real-time correlation functions of light scattered from the interface. By this method, fluctuations with lifetimes of several seconds may be observed. The phenomena is basically due to the interaction of the radiation with excitations (Ripplons) within the interface, which have properties similar to those of capillary gravitational surface waves. These investigations and others may all be carried out using a c.w. argon ion laser as source, a Fabry–Pérot interferometer or frequency analyser as a spectrometer, and standard auxiliary equipment to detect and record the scattering information.

## 10.6. *Other applications*

There are a great many other areas in which the particular properties of the inert gases make them suitable for a specific purpose. In nuclear physics, for example they are used as filling gases for ionization chambers, proportional and Geiger–Müller counters, because they do not form negative ions by electron attachment. Liquid helium and xenon are used in bubble chambers.

A bubble chamber is a device which detects radiation by the ionization produced in a superheated liquid, which causes minute bubbles along its track. It is similar in many ways to the older Wilson cloud chamber, but because of the greater density of the detection medium, more ionizing events take place per unit path length. The advantage of using xenon in a bubble chamber is that it has a high atomic number and therefore the electrons in the outer shell are relatively more easily detached, producing ions which act as nuclei for the formation of bubbles. Particles which cause little ionization, such as $\gamma$-photons and neutral mesons, can thus be detected.

Even in an engineering field such as jet propulsion, the inert gases are proving to be useful research materials. For example, tubes containing argon are used to study the ionization of gases by shock waves. By rupturing a diaphragm, a wave is made to travel through the tube at speeds ranging up to ten times the velocity of sound. The passage of the waves raises the temperature for an instant to $\sim 5000$ K—high enough to initiate measurable ionization in the argon. The rate at which the argon approaches its equilibrium ionization is measured by its absorption and reflections of a probing microwave beam.

Studies of this nature are valuable because conditions in the shock tube are similar to those found in jet propulsion devices. The knowledge gained by performing experiments with simple substances such as argon leads to a better understanding of the basic mechanisms which occur in these devices and thus results in improved designs.

There are of course a great number of other applications of the inert gases in science and technology. Cook lists over 200 uses in his book (see 'suggested reading' list), but only a selection have been given here to avoid this chapter becoming merely a catalogue. One thing is clear: whereas as little as two decades ago the inert gases were regarded as dull and rather useless materials, today they play an important role in an increasingly wide range of scientific and industrial applications.

## basic thermodynamics

SOME knowledge of elementary thermodynamic principles is necessary for an understanding of much of this book and the following is intended to serve as an introduction (or revision) to those unfamiliar with the subject. Macroscopic thermodynamics is concerned with relationships between thermodynamic co-ordinates used to describe a system, for example, temperature, pressure and volume. The object of microscopic or statistical thermodynamics is to relate atomic and molecular properties, for example lattice spacing and intermolecular potential, to the bulk thermodynamic co-ordinates. The properties discussed in this book are nearly all ' static ' and it is assumed that bulk properties or averaged statistical properties are constant during the period of observation. (An obvious exception to this are the ' fluctuation phenomena ' near critical points discussed in Chapter 7.)

The aim is to obtain the normal equation of state (e.g. $pV = RT$ for a perfect gas), and also the ' caloric ' equation of state, i.e. an equation relating to the total energy of a system to other thermodynamic properties. The former on its own is not adequate to fully define a thermodynamic system since it does not indicate whether or not it is in stable equilibrium. The most convenient method of discussing these properties is by introducing the thermodynamic concepts of internal energy, entropy and free energy.

Suppose that a volume of gas is heated slightly by an amount $\Delta Q$ so that it expands, doing a small amount of work $\Delta W$. Some of the heat will have been converted into work, and some may have gone into changing the kinetic or potential energy of the molecules by an amount $\Delta U$. According to the first law of thermodynamics (which is an application of the law of conservation of energy)

$$\Delta Q = \Delta U + \Delta W$$

By introducing the idea of an internal energy function $U$, this equation essentially extends the principle of the conservation of energy to include heat. If the work done is expanding the gas by a volume $\Delta V$ at constant pressure, then $\Delta Q = \Delta U + p\Delta V$.

One can define another quantity $S$, the entropy, in terms of the change produced in a system by heating it reversibly at constant temperature $T$. (A reversible reaction is one for which all stages are in equilibrium, i.e. one can stop at any point.) Under these conditions, the entropy change

$\Delta S$ is given by

$$\Delta S = \Delta Q / T$$

Thus entropy is a function of the thermodynamic co-ordinates, and is related to the energy content of system. Its properties are as follows. For all reversible adiabatic changes $\Delta S = 0$, for reversible isothermal changes $\Delta S = \Delta Q / T$, and for all non-adiabatic, irreversible changes $\Delta S > \Delta Q / T$. This is essentially the second law of thermodynamics: i.e. $\Delta S \geqslant 0$. Alternatively the first and second laws can be combined as $T . \Delta S \geqslant \Delta U + p \Delta V$.

An important feature of entropy is that it is related to the microscopic order in a system. In fact, as the entropy of a system increases, the molecular disorder also increases. This link between the macroscopic and microscopic may be expressed as

$$S = k \ln \Omega$$

where $\Omega$ is a statistical quantity describing the total number of possible configurations of the molecules in the system. If $\Omega$ can be calculated by statistical mechanics, then the relation describing the first and second laws given above provides a convenient bridge between $\Omega$ and observed properties such as $p$ and $V$.

Some idea of the link between entropy and order may be obtained by considering the number of ways in which one can place three identical balls in a box. If the box is only large enough to accept the three balls, then only one distinct distribution may be obtained and this corresponds to perfect order. If the box is enlarged, however, the number of possible distributions increases, $\Omega$ is larger because of the greater number of possible macrostates and the system is more disordered. The entropy is greater because $S = k \ln \Omega$. Applying similar considerations to solids, liquids and gases, it can be seen, for example, that a solid is much more ordered than a gas because the molecular configurations are greatly restricted, and that increasing the disorder (heating a mole of solid until it vapourizes), involves increasing the entropy of the system.

There are two other thermodynamic functions that are very useful. The Helmholtz free energy $F$ is defined as

$$F = U - TS$$

and the Gibbs free energy $G$ is defined as

$$G = U + pV - TS$$

The change in the Helmholtz free energy $\Delta F$ is equal to the work done on a system $-p \Delta V$ for reversible isothermal changes. It is important from a statistical mechanical standpoint because one can calculate $F$ as a function of volume and temperature and hence deter-

164

mine the equation of state and the entropy of a system from $p = -(\partial F/\partial V)_T$ and $S = -(\partial F/\partial T)_V$. [The partial differentiation $(\partial A/\partial B)_C$ means that the function $A$ is differentiated with respect to $B$, assuming that $C$ is a constant.] A system at constant volume and temperature tends to the lowest value of $F$ permitted by the equation of state. This has interesting consequences. For example, it is found that a crystal in equilibrium near its melting point contains a number of vacancies, even though this increases its internal energy by an amount $\Delta U$. The reason for this is that the presence of vacancies increases the microscopic disorder in the crystal (§ 5.4), hence the number of possible configurations or microstates, and therefore the entropy $\Delta S$. As long as $T\Delta S > \Delta U$, then the introduction of vacancies will make the crystal more stable since $\Delta F = \Delta U - T\Delta S$ is negative and hence $F$ decreases.

Similarly for reversible isothermal changes $\Delta G = V\Delta p$, and for all processes that take place at constant pressure and temperature, a system tends to the lowest value of $G$ permitted by the equation of state. The Gibbs free energy is useful when considering phase equilibrium since phase changes can be considered as taking place isothermally and iso-barically. The stable phase is the one for which $G$ is a minimum, i.e. the solid–liquid melting point marks the temperature below which $G_{SOL} < G_{LIQ}$.

*Suggestions for further reading:*

There are several inexpensive books that would provide useful background reading to this volume. For example, *Gases, Liquids and Solids* by D. Tabor (Penguin Books) discusses many of the concepts used here in greater detail. *Equilibrium Thermodynamics* by C. J. Adkins (McGraw-Hill) gives a very clear account of elementary thermodynamic principles. *The Liquid State* by J. A. Pryde (Hutchinson), and *The Elementary Science of Metals* (Wykeham Science Series) would be helpful in understanding the chapters on the liquid and solid states.

For a more detailed account of the properties of the inert gases, readers with access to a college library are referred to the book and articles listed below. These all give extensive references to original work.

Cook, G. A. *Argon, Helium and the Rare Gases*, vols I and II (Interscience).
Bewilogua, L. and Cladun, C. 1968. 'Condensed inert gases', *Contemporary Physics*, vol 9, p. 277.
Smith, B. L. 1969. 'Critical point phenomena', *Contemporary Physics*, vol 10, p. 305.
Smith, B. L. 1970. 'Inert gas crystals', *Contemporary Physics*, vol 11, p. 125.
Smith, B. L. 1971. 'Applications of the inert gases', *Contemporary Physics*, vol 12, p. 105.

# INDEX

168

170

# THE WYKEHAM SCIENCE SERIES

# THE WYKEHAM TECHNOLOGICAL SERIES

All orders and requests for inspection copies should be sent to the appropriate agents. A list of agents and their territories is given on the verso of the title page of this book.